# MARCO POLO

KT-239-093

Lincolnshire

**Tips**

# DUBROVNIK &
# DALMATIAN COAST

Austria — Hungary
Villach
Slovenia
Ljubljana — Zagreb
IT
Trieste — Rijeka — Croatia — Serbia
Croatian — Bosnia
coast / — Herzegovina
Dalmatia — Sarajevo
Ancona — Split
— MONTE-
*Adriatic* — NEGRO
Dubrovnik

The best Insider Tips → p. 4

INSIDER TIP

Best of ... → p. 6

Zadar region → p. 32

Split region → p. 54

## SYMBOLS

| | |
|---|---|
| INSIDER TIP | Insider Tip |
| ★ | Highlight |
| ●●●● | Best of ... |
| ☼ | Scenic view |
| 🌱 | Responsible travel: for eco-logical or fair trade aspects |

## PRICE CATEGORIES HOTELS

*Expensive* over 1,100 kunas

*Moderate* 600 – 1,100 kunas

*Budget* under 600 kunas

Prices per night during the peak season for a double room, based on two people sharing, incl. breakfast

## PRICE CATEGORIES RESTAURANTS

*Expensive* over 260 kunas

*Moderate* 190 – 260 kunas

*Budget* under 190 kunas

Prices for a typical meal on the restaurant's menu consisting of starter, entree, dessert and one drink

On the cover: Makarska Riviera: p. 65 | Vis' hidden treasures: p. 98

# CONTENTS

Dubrovnik region → p. 78

Trips & tours → p. 98

Sports & activities → p. 104

Road atlas → p. 128

**DID YOU KNOW?**

**MAPS IN THE GUIDEBOOK**
(130 A1) Page numbers and coordinates refer to the road atlas
(0) Site/address located off the map. Coordinates are also given for places that are not marked on the road atlas
Street maps of Dubrovnik, Split, Trogir and Zadar can be found inside the back cover

**INSIDE BACK COVER:**
**PULL-OUT MAP →**

**PULL-OUT MAP** 🗺
(🗺 A–B 2–3) Refers to the removable pull-out map

# The best MARCO POLO Insider Tips

## Our top 15 Insider Tips

**INSIDER TIP** **Temporary lighthouse keeper**

For those who like solitude: the only people you have to share Veli Rat lighthouse on Dugi otok with are the tenants of the other apartment; you will usually have the endless beach completely to yourself → **p. 37**

**INSIDER TIP** **Gourmet temple**

Šibenik's well-to-do society has fully embraced Pelegrini's fusion cuisine. Chef Rudi combines Dalmatian traditions with modern culinary skills and serves up the result amidst exposed stone walls → **p. 40**

**INSIDER TIP** **Hiking with distant views**

There's a panoramic hiking trail on Pašman that winds its way through rocks, sage and rosemary for 24 km (14.9 mi) → **p. 45**

**INSIDER TIP** **Specialities from the grill**

The rustic Konoba Tomić on Brač serves well-seasoned meat, home-made bread and home-grown vegetables → **p. 57**

**INSIDER TIP** **Sculpted stone**

Dražen Jakšić was a hugely talented sculptor, who made the most magnificent sculptures out of the famous Brač Rock → **p. 58**

**INSIDER TIP** **When the lavender is in bloom**

An experience of the scented kind: between July and September the island of Hvar is dyed purple: this is the flowering season of the lavender, which fills the air with an aromatic scent (photo r.) → **p. 63**

**INSIDER TIP** **Casual lounge**

The beach club of the popular Carpe Diem bar is the place to be seen in Hvar. In addition the wooden platforms and ladders spare you the laborious route across the rocks into the water → **p. 63**

**INSIDER TIP** **Where the Greek ships ran ashore**

Several ancient trading vessels carrying amphorae sunk off Cavtat; diving down to the wrecks is an unforgettable experience → **p. 80**

## INSIDER TIP Oysters and wine

While you are eating oysters at the simple Kamenice buffet in Dubrovnik's old town, the market women next door barter with customers about vegetable prices → **p. 83**

## INSIDER TIP In sea kayaks around the old town

Unusual perspectives of Dubrovnik's fortifications: take a sea kayak around the city walls and to the island of Lokrum (photo l.) → **p. 85**

## INSIDER TIP Dubrovnik from above

As if planned on a drawing board, Dubrovnik lies at your feet when with the help of the cable-car you conquer the local mountain, 412-metre Mount Srd → **p. 87**

## INSIDER TIP Herbal drinks from an organic farmer

Everything Mate cooks and presses at his agrotourism site on Korčula tastes delicious and comes fresh from the field or the garden, and it's all organic of course! → **p. 92**

## INSIDER TIP Wreck in paradise

Camping Adriatic is the name of anw enchanting spot on the Pelješac peninsula: built on terraces right by the sea, it is manageably small, simple and wonderfully quiet. Divers will be excited by the wreck in the turquoise bay → **p. 96**

## INSIDER TIP The dream bay

Admittedly it is quite an effort to get down into this hidden bay on the island of Vis, and even more of an effort to climb back up, but the pebble bay of Uvala Stiniva, surrounded almost entirely by steep rock walls, is a consummately beautiful sea of pale turquoise → **p. 99**

## INSIDER TIP Seafaring tradition

Fishermen and merchants used to navigate the Adriatic in traditional boats. At the end of September, on Michaelmas Day, they gather in Murter for the Latinsko idro regatta – a wonderful sight! → **p. 113**

# BEST OF ...

**FOR FREE**

● *View of the Kornati archipelago*
There is a winding road leading up from Lake Vrana into the Biokovo mountains to the Kamenjak viewpoint. The view over the small Kornati islands scattered in the sea is stunning and completely free of charge → p. 36

● *Glagolica on Pašman*
At the moment the Benedictines of SS. Cosmas & Damian near Tkon are still not charging an entrance fee to show off their beautifully situated abbey and Gothic church, whose portal bears Glagolitic inscriptions → p. 46

● *Fresh fish from the fish market*
Every morning the same thing happens in the fish market hall in Zadar: the fishermen deliver their catch and the dealers pile up sardines, sort through octopuses, decorate crayfish and arrange crabs into pyramids. It's a sight fit for the video camera and as an added bonus, this show is completely free → p. 50

● *Swimming for free*
In and around Dubrovnik's old town, bathing spots are rare: beach clubs charge entrance fees or the beaches can only be accessed by ferry. One tip for those wanting to take a cool dip: on the southern edge of the old town, in Od Margarite street, there is a hole in the city wall. It is possible to climb down from the rock on the other side and start swimming → p. 85

● *Stari Grad Plain*
A Unesco World Heritage Site for free: Stari Grad Plain on the island of Hvar is used for farming, and been for several thousand years. The low walls that border the fields are divided into chora, set up by the ancient Greeks. That is what makes this valley so unique → p. 64

● *Medieval picture book*
You could spend several hours gazing at the portal of Trogir Cathedral without running out of new discoveries. The Old and New Testaments were chiselled into the stone, as if in a frenzy. They can be seen perfectly well from the square without paying a cent (photo) → p. 74

◐●●● Dots in guidebook refer to 'Best of ...' tips

# ONLY IN DALMATIA
## Unique experiences

● *No boundary between land and sea*

The fact that the Dalmatian island world consists of peaks whose mountains were submerged 15,000 years ago is nowhere so palpable as on the island of Dugi otok → p. 36

● *Golden Cape*

It is one of Brač's landmarks and adorns almost every tourist brochure. Zlatni Rat, a horn-shaped beach near the town of Bol, occasionally changes the direction in which it points, depending on the whims of the wind → p. 55

● *Sweet sounds*

When the people of Dalmatia sing, then they usually do so a cappella and with many parts. The whole of Dalmatia watches when the best klapa choirs go head to head in the town of Omiš → p. 68

● *The navel of the city*

The cathedral square in Korčula and its cathedral, bishop's palace and smoothly polished paving is an architectural ensemble that can be found in many Dalmatian cities, yet it has its very own character → p. 90

● *Under a cast iron bell*

Dalmatian cuisine is traditionally associated with grilled dishes. Vanity Fair affirmed this perception when it crowned Konoba Pol Murvu on the island of Vis the best grill in the world. However, Dalmatia's actual secret is its cast iron peka, under which lamb or squid are gently roasted with onions, potatoes and vegetables – hugely delicious, and also on the menu at Konoba Pol Murvu → p. 99

● *Walking in Plitvice Lakes National Park*

Intense colours and cool air provide a contrast to the coast. Waterfalls connect lakes located at different levels; trout flit through the water, while dragonflies dance over the green surface (photo) → p. 102

● *Island hopping*

From one of the Elaphiti Islands to another: an old ferry leaves in the morning, laden with cattle, washing machines and the mail, stopping off at Koločep, Lopud and Šipan. In the evening it returns to Dubrovnik. Between setting off and returning lie Mediterranean islands and sandy beaches, waiting to be enjoyed → p. 111

ONLY IN

# BEST OF ...

● **Reliquaries, goblets and panels**
In Zadar's museum of sacred art, known as 'The Gold and Silver of Zadar', millennia-old church treasures shine brightly, fighting off dreary thoughts produced by bad weather → **p. 48**

● **Shopping in the emperor's palace**
Diocletian's Palace in Split's old town was diverted from its intended use over the centuries and now features souvenir stalls. But when the weather is bad, this is a wonderful place to go shopping (photo) → **p. 70**

● **From the Roman mausoleum to the cathedral**
The site was initially occupied by the mausoleum of Diocletian, who died in Split in the 4th century; it was later surrounded by the magnificent Split Cathedral, St Duje. Look for clues: What is Roman? What is Christian? → **p. 71**

● **Visiting a master**
On a hot day many are drawn more to the sea and less to the suburbs of Split, where Croatia's most famous sculptor, Ivan Mestrović, set up his studio. However, when it's raining, going to see his works, which are monumental, disturbing and fascinating, will bring exciting insights into 20th century art → **p. 73**

● **History in the Fifth Dimension**
The Visia Dubrovnik Theatrum presents visitors with a virtual tour of Dubrovnik's history; it is a well-done, entertaining show with special effects and 5-D animation → **p. 83**

● **Among sea dogs**
These days the colourful sails of the sailboarders dominate the strait between Korčula and Orebić; in the past proud ships departed from here to sail to destinations all over the world. The maritime museum reveals just how significant shipping was for Orebić → **p. 96**

RAIN

# RELAX AND CHILL OUT
## Take it easy and spoil yourself

● *Dancing sails*
Hillsides sprinkled with maquis frame the elongated Telašćica Bay, rounded hills peek out of the water and white sails are filled with wind. Could there be anything more relaxing than spending a day here? → **p. 38**

● *Contemplation with the Franciscans*
When the town of Hvar gets particularly crowded, when the in-crowd is partying in Carpe Diem and the yacht parade is in full swing in the harbour, then the nearby Franciscan monastery is one way to escape from the hustle and bustle → **p. 62**

● *Decadently Roman*
Roman bathing traditions provided the model for the Spa of Diocletian in Le Meridien Lav near Split: caldarium, tepidarium and the aroma grotto guarantee relaxation, using all of the skills of Roman bath design. After a traditional massage, the only things missing for absolute bliss are a toga and the imperial crown → **p. 72**

● *A magical place*
The time of day and the position of the sun have to be right for this boat trip, because then the water in the Blue Grotto on Biševo shimmers in such an intense turquoise that it feels like being in an ice palace → **p. 77**

● *The song of the waves*
The sea organ must be one of the loveliest spots in Zadar – sit on the steps of this acoustic artwork and listen to the melodies the sea brings to life in it (photo) → **p. 48**

● *Taking time out*
Regardless of whether you prefer Lopud or Šipan, both of these Elaphiti Islands possess one thing aplenty: peace and quiet. Rent a room in one of the elegant, small family hotels and wait until the day-trippers have left the island. Then you will be alone with just a few skippers and the people who live here → **p. 88**

# INTRODUCTION

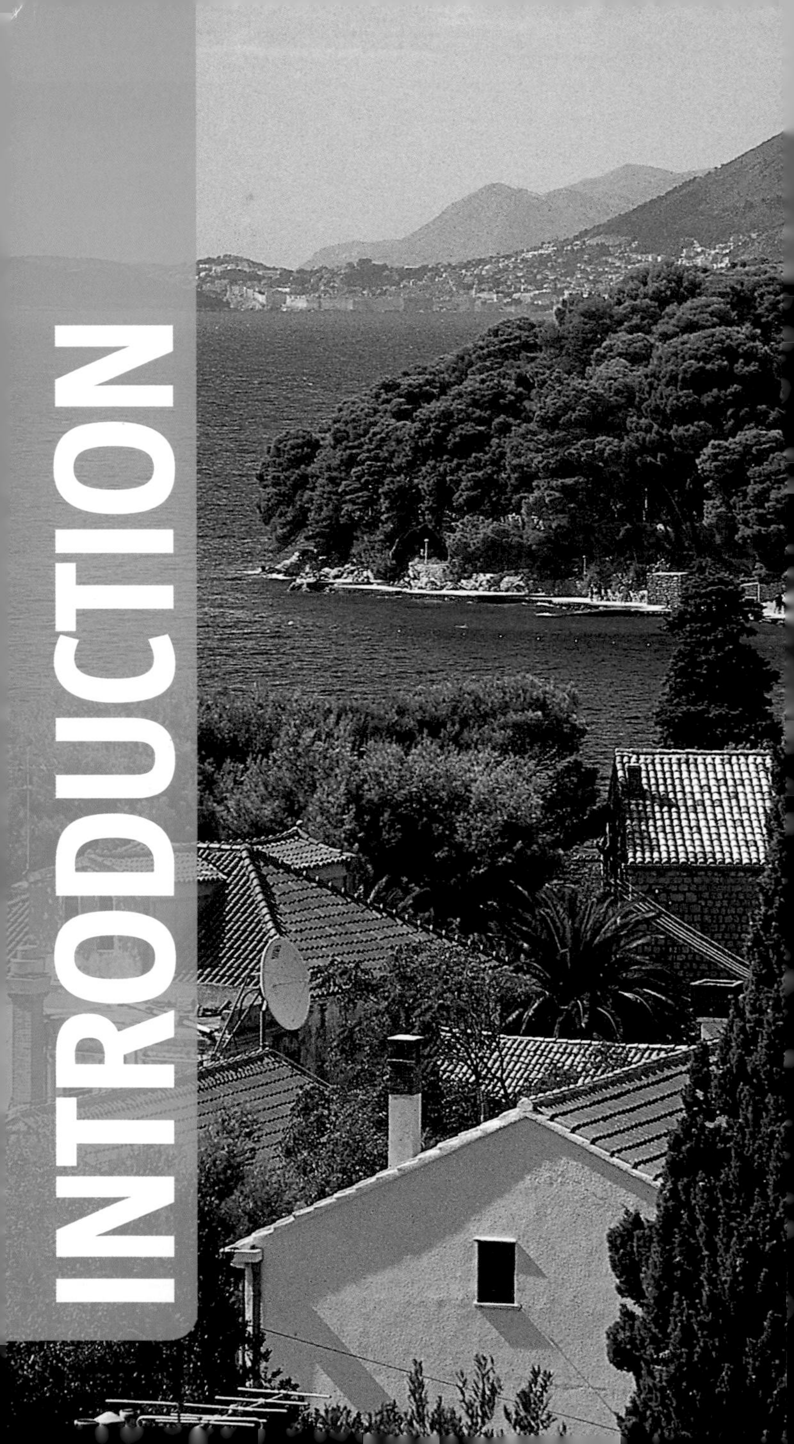

# DISCOVER THE DALMATIAN COAST!

Imagine the following: 1777 kilometres (1100 miles) of coastline, off which there are a total of 1184 islands. There are large ones such as Brač and tiny ones such as Lokrum, inhabited ones and inhospitable rocky reefs, lavishly green ones and ones only suitable for sheep grazing. Some are given a jagged appearance by their countless bays, while others are lined by beaches. An absolute dream destination!

Most of the islands lie directly off the Dalmatian coast in the Adriatic. It is not surprising that this coastline is one of Europe's most beautiful sailing spots and a holiday landscape whose diverse appeals, changing moods, ruggedness and charm will create lasting memories.

The peaks of the Dinaric Alps, which reach an altitude of 1700 metres (1860 yd), create a dramatic barrier to inland Croatia. Squeezed between the range and the sea are coastal towns, while grapes, oranges, olives and palm trees flourish, sheltered from the wind by the mountains. This unusual landscape is still quite young. The coastal range was only flooded after the most recent ice age; the peaks were transformed into

Photo: View over the roofs of Cavtat

Idyllic, crystal-clear water, a small bay for swimming and the shade of trees

islands, the valleys into straits. When travelling by coastal ferry, this process of formation is particularly visible on the trip through the archipelago of Zadar: the islands of Ugljan and Dugi otok lie on either side, and in between is the small island of Iž.

## The people's lives are oriented towards the sea

About the coastal ferry in general: complete at least one day-leg, as there is no nicer way to get to know this coastline, where the boundary between water and land seems to disappear. On a boat trip it also becomes very evident how all the people here live facing the sea. The many little ports, characterized by Venetian influences, seem to have been constructed following a single principle: the most beautiful side is to be seen from the water. The wide open expanse, faraway places and the longing to depart to different shores are constantly present here. This sen-

**1st millennium BC – 2nd century AD**
The Illyrians, Greeks and finally the Romans settle in Dalmatia and found trading posts

**6th – 10th centuries**
Dalmatia is Byzantine; Slavs immigrate into the area; founding of the first Croatian kingdom

**from the 12th century onwards**
Dalmatia subject to Venice. From the mid-15th century Ottoman troops threaten the coast

**1797 – 1918**
Venetian rule comes to an end under Napoleon. The same thing happens to Ragusa in 1808. Austria takes over the legacy of these trading powers

timent is reflected most beautifully in Dalmatian music, the traditional songs of the klapa choirs. The sentiment can also be felt in the pop-music versions by Tomislav Bralić, probably the most popular interpreter of modern Dalmatian music. Sadly, his versions often turn out to be pure schmaltz.

Many legends are told about the formation of the Dalmatian coast, of God's wonderful creation in this otherwise incredibly harsh landscape. Did He re-

## Deep gorges and gurgling rivers

ally cry on the bare rocks, whereupon His tears turned into islands? In any case, He was also generous to the land behind the mountain ridge: there are deep gorges with rivers winding their way through them, such as in Paklenica National Park and Cetina Gorge, in Krka National Park, where the Krka River gurgles over limestone steps, and in the enchanting landscape of Plitvice Lakes National Park, which is also a Unesco World Heritage Site. If you like hiking and climbing, getting out into the hills on a mountain bike or going kayaking, then this nature reserve and the others will be just the thing.

In the past the Dalmatians were great seafarers. They sailed all the way to America in their boats. These days they are still equipping oil platforms with small, agile lifeboats. In the shipyards they convert fishing boats into leisure craft. The great era of shipbuilding is over, however. Croatia's economy, particularly the industrial sector, has experienced a dramatic nose-dive since the country separated from Yugoslavia; it has proved a real struggle for the economy to get back on its feet. Unemployment is

**from 1918**
Croats, Serbs and Slovenes found the kingdom of Yugoslavia, which surrenders to Germany in World War II (1941)

**1939 – 45**
Partisan groups fight against the German Wehrmacht

**1945**
Founding of the 'Federal Republic of Yugoslavia' under the leadership of Prime Minister Josip Broz Tito and the Communist Party

**1980**
After Tito's death the multi-ethnic state sees the growth of nationalism and an economic crisis

high, particularly among young people. Tourism, however, is booming, which makes Dalmatia one of the richest regions in the country, if not the richest.

What do the Croatians dream of? Family, work, security: in this they are no different from most other Europeans. Croatia had to spend a long time working on goals such as getting stronger, being recognized in Europe and joining the EU. It was not the country's unknown culture, or the ailing economy, that caused Croatia to be excluded from the EU for so long. Instead it was ugly terms such as 'corruption' and 'war crimes'. The entanglement between politics, the justice system and business was an inheritance of the communist multi-ethnic state of Yugoslavia. Only in the last ten years has cutting this Gordian knot been a major goal. The story is similar when it comes to dealing with Croatian war crimes that took place during the Yugoslav war. It was not until the highly decorated general Ante Gotovina was handed over to the tribunal in The Hague in 2005 that the world saw that Croatia was serious about this issue.

## 2000 years of history in a small space

It is not just the past 25 years that have been eventful. Dalmatia's history has been eventful right from the start. In the colonnaded courtyard in Diocletian's Palace in Split, you are intimately surrounded by nearly two thousand years of history. By the columns and arches of a Roman palace. By a pre-Romanesque stone relief in the baptistery, evidence of an era during which Croatia was an independent kingdom and during which it opened up to Christianity. By Gothic carvings on church doors, which were made when Venice subjugated almost the whole of Dalmatia. By the Baroque frenzy of the cathedral's interior, which celebrates Dalmatia's golden age. The modern era is also represented here. The people of Split like to while away an hour in the pleasant Café Luxor, enjoying an espresso and reading the paper.

Only the ancient Greeks failed to immortalize themselves here, but they left their mark elsewhere. On the sea floor, for example, where hundreds of amphorae from sunken merchant vessels provide special motifs for divers in addition to the already biodiverse underwater world. The ancient Greeks also left their mark on the island of Hvar, or, to be precise, on Stari Grad Plain, where the farmers have, for the past 2000

**1991 – 95**
Croatia declares its independence, attack by the Yugoslav army

**1995**
Croats, Serbs and Bosnians sign a peace treaty

**2009**
With the election of Jadranka Kosor, the pragmatic, EU-oriented forces assert themselves in the Croatian Democratic Union (HDZ), which has a tendency towards excessive nationalism

**2010**
In the border dispute regarding the Gulf of Piran, the Slovenes and Croats agree to call in international arbitration; Croatia's EU membership comes a step closer

Cavtat: palm trees line the waterfront promenade of Croatia's southernmost seaside resort

years, continuously used the boundaries set by the Greek colonists in around 400 BC. Stari Grad Plain is a Unesco World Heritage Site, as is Diocletian's Palace in Split, the wonderful Šibenik Cathedral, the Romanesque old town of Trogir and the old town of Dubrovnik. As the Republic of Ragusa, the city managed to withstand the Venetians and the Turks alike, usually through cunning and skilled negotiation. Today Dubrovnik has to withstand the crowds of people that flood in through its old city wall every summer from aeroplanes and cruise ships, because the city is one of the top destinations in Europe and a must for all globetrotters. The city and its people put up with this patiently and elegantly, like the inhabitants of Hvar, the town that is popularly compared to Marbella and Ibiza. The romantic little town on the island of lavender is up at the top of the to-do list of celebs and starlets.

The Croats have invented all sorts of things: torpedoes, biros and ties, and if anyone deserves credit for inventing hospitality, then it ought to be this nation with its open arms and hearts. Be-

**The insatiable desire to celebrate every occasion**

ing helpful and open and having infinite energy to celebrate any event, never mind how small, are characteristics all visitors will see plenty of evidence of. A Croatian encounter, which naturally also includes a lavish meal, usually starts and ends with a glass of schnapps – something that those from more northerly climes don't always cope well with in warm temperatures. But join in anyway, you only have to have a few sips!

Go on a journey of discovery! The tranquil and often harsh beauty of the islands and bays, the crystal-clear water, the romantic backdrop of medieval ports, fancy restaurants behind rustic walls and finally a beach lounge lit by flares: all these things await.

# WHAT'S HOT

## 1 Art, naturally!

**Natural material** Ive Kora creates faces and landscapes using the wood of olive trees *(Postira, www.ivekora.com, photo)*. Stone and metal on the other hand are the natural starting materials for Matko Mijić's sculptures. One of the places his works can be seen is *Galerija Kula (Trg Kralja Tomislava bb 21, Split)*. *Galerija Freska* exhibits works created by Ante Mandarić from terracotta and wood *(Plinarska 49, Split, www.galerija-freska.com)*.

## For animal-lovers 2

**Take away** Until recently vegetarian restaurants were almost unthinkable in this region. Now, however, a new dining trend is flourishing in Croatia. The menu of *Nishta* is one-hundred-percent vegetarian *(Prijeko b.b., Dubrovnik, www.nishtarestaurant.com)*. Veggie-lovers will find what they are looking for in *Makrovega (Leština 2, Split, www.makrovega.hr)*. *Kalumela* is not just vegetarian. The shop also serves vegan take-aways, which even make do without white flour and additives *(Dormaldova 7, Split)*.

## 3 Fashion forward

**Designer eye** Fashion newcomers have put the region on the map with their designs. Femininity is trumps in *Envy Room (Atelier La Perla, Svačićeva 5, Split)*. The designs of *Modna kuća MAK* are playful and sensuous *(Cro-a-Porter, Široka ulica 18, Zadar)*. In *Ronchi Hat Factory* extravagant hats are lovingly created *(Lučarica 2, Dubrovnik, photo)*, and *Croatian Fashion Design* is the place to go for native stars such as Igor Dalaš and Ivana Zanko *(Zlatarska 3, Dubrovnik)*.

# First steps

*A new approach to environmentalism* Brač is a real model region, because the island is striving for independence – when it comes to energy. The goal of the Easy project is to use only regional and renewable energies on Brač *(www.easyaction.eu, photo)*. This movement also includes everyday projects, such as the green launderette in Split. *Bijela košulja* (white jacket) only uses green laundry soaps, perfect for holiday-home visitors and backpackers *(Kneza Višeslava 6)*. *Box Coffee Shop* goes a step further *(Poljicka cesta 39, Split)*. This café does not have paper newspapers. Instead guests can get their morning news fix for free on an iPad, but whether this is beneficial to the environment or not Is another matter.

# Archaeology underwater

*Good prospects* Diving is not a new sport, but underwater sightseeing with archaeology experts is. Excursions like this are offered by *Diving Center Cavtat (in Hotel Croatia, Frankopanska 10, Cavtat, www. divingcentercavtat.hr)*. The International Centre for Underwater Archaeology (ICUA) in Zadar has a list on its website of the region's diving clubs with a licence to dive in the cultural heritage sites. In addition the ICUA gives lectures and seminars on the subject. This way visitors can quickly become experts themselves *(icua.hr, photo)*. Those who fear deep water will have no problems on Silba. Relics of the past were found off this island's coast at a depth of just 2 m. There are now plans to set up an underwater museum for snorkellers.

# IN A NUTSHELL

## ADRIA MAGISTRALE

This technical feat, built under Tito, runs from Ankaran (Slovenia) to Ulcinj (Montenegro) and is the main artery of the Adriatic tourist industry. As one of the most beautiful scenic roads in Europe, the Adria Magistrale connects holiday regions along more than 1200 km (756 mi) of Croatian coastline. At dizzying heights, it nestles close to the steep, rugged rocks, winds around estuaries and bays, through gardens and over scree. Wonderful views open up of the blue sea, green islands, bizarre rocks and Mediterranean towns and villages.

The particularly dangerous sections were recently made safer. In addition the new motorway from Zagreb to Dubrovnik via Split, which currently stops around 120 km (75 mi) outside of Dubrovnik, provides relief for the Magistrale. During the peak holiday season the winding road still has a heightened risk of accidents because of the many overtaking manoeuvres by car drivers trying to get ahead of the caravans and lorries.

## BEACHES

Croatia's coastline possesses countless rocky bays, but only few pebble beaches, let alone sandy ones. This special topography has the advantage that the water is unmuddied by sand, making it virtually crystal clear. The disadvantage, however, lies in the fact that in order to get into the water, swimmers often have to navigate sharp rocks that are the preferred hiding place of sea urchins. These

## Bays, islands and dolphins: facts worth knowing about Renaissance art, lighthouses and Dalmatia's fascinating natural environment

are two good reasons to wear shoes in the water, because injuries caused by their spines, which have hooks on them, can be very painful and can become inflamed. In many places the municipal administrations have addressed this problem by running concrete platforms and ladders into the sea. This solution is not pretty but it is certainly practical.

## CRAVAT

In the Thirty Years War, in around 1635, a Croatian regiment came to Paris to support Louis XIII's troops. The 6000 uniformed men attracted great attention everywhere because they wore colourful cloths around their necks, tied with special knots. These neckerchiefs, made of coarse linen for simple soldiers and fine cotton and silk for officers, excited the French so much that they made cravats a fashion accessory of their civilian clothing. This invention, named after its homeland, soon became haute couture. It developed into the necktie, which has become established around the world, primarily in formal men's wear.

# DATES & FACTS

The Republic of Croatia, with the most beautiful coastline along the Adriatic, boasting far more than a thousand islands and reefs, its natural resources, such as gas and oil, its fertile soils, its beautiful landscape as well as its rich cultural and historical heritage, lies between the Mediterranean and the Danube and covers an area of 56,538 sq km (21,829 sq mi).

The country is called *Hrvatska* in its native language. Its capital is Zagreb (more than 1 million inhabitants). 90 percent of Croatia's 4.4 million inhabitants are Croats by descent. 90 percent of the population are also members of the Roman Catholic church. The country bordering Croatia to the north is Slovenia, the neighbours to the east are Hungary, Serbia and Bosnia-Herzegovina, and to the south, Montenegro.

The Republic of Croatia is a parliamentary democracy. Head of government Jadranka Kosor, from the conservative HDZ party, is pursuing pragmatic policies aimed at reconciliation with the former Yugoslav states; the independent president, Ivo Josipović, elected in 2010, stands for this new political style without the nationalist overtones previously cultivated by Franjo Tudjman, the founder of the state. A unitary state, Croatia is divided into 20 provinces *(Županije)*. The goal of the 2001 administrative reform has been decentralization and the strengthening of local autonomy.

In 2009 Croatia became a full member of Nato; membership of the EU, planned for the same year, had to be delayed once again. The reasons for this are the continuing entanglement

Rugged bays line the coast around Dubrovnik

of politics and business, the hesitant co-operation with the UN war crimes tribunal, as well as the escalating border conflict with EU member Slovenia regarding sovereign waters in the Gulf of Piran, which, after serious polemics on both sides, has finally been put to an international arbitrating body. Croatia can now hope to be part of the next EU enlargement.

# ECONOMY & TOURISM

Croatia is in the middle of a difficult transformation, from a state-run to a privately run economy. This process is not going smoothly everywhere. The international financial crisis hit the Croatian economy, which had just began to recover after the war and the country's independence, particularly badly. 66 percent of the country's gross domestic product comes from the service sector; but in recent years profits from this sector fell by almost six percent, while industrial production (previously 28 percent of the GDP) decreased by almost ten percent. Unemployment went up to ten percent. Since this collapse the economy has seen gentle but constant growth, not least thanks to tourism, which contributes 20 percent to the country's GDP.

# FLORA

Brittle karst in all colour nuances, ranging from snow white to dark grey, dominates the landscape of the Croatian coastline. It is the frugal plants that put on their floral displays on this arid, inhospitable stony terrain, bringing the rugged rocks to life. In spring the rocks are covered in yellow gorse, while lavender and sage cover the scree fields in a blanket of lilac during the summer months. When the autumn comes around, the bright red fruits of the strawberry tree stand out from the maquis.

The omnipresent maquis grows on arid rocky soils in bright sunlight to form low-growing, luxuriant evergreen shrubs. It has adapted perfectly to the Mediterranean conditions. Butterflies and bees are attracted by the savoury scent of rosemary, thyme and oregano. Shade can be found under holm oaks, laurel trees, pines and cypresses.

The vineyards and olive groves, on the other hand, are manmade. Fertile humus gathers in valley bottoms (polje). Lemons, oranges, kiwis, melons and peaches as well as onions, beans, tomatoes, cucumbers, peppers and artichokes grow well in it.

# JURAJ DALMATINAC

Few artists have shaped Dalmatia's art and architecture as much as Juraj Dalmatinac, who was born in Zadar in around 1420. He designed and built the town of Pag on the island of the same name, he was significantly involved in building the Cathedral of St James in Šibenik and he worked in Split, Zadar and Dubrovnik. Dalmatinac learned his trade under famous master-builders in Venice. That is also where he came into contact with the emerging Renaissance, whose decorative elements and architectural designs he took home with him to Dalmatia, thus bringing about the end of the Gothic period.

An all-round genius, he worked as a town planner, an architect and a sculptor. Among his masterpieces are the apses of Šibenik Cathedral, which are decorated with the heads of famous citizens, and the relief of the Flagellation of Christ in Split Cathedral. The way he dealt with stone as his construction material, which was abundantly available in Dalmatia, was positively revolutionary. While his Italian counterparts were constructing barrel vaults out of wood and brick, he developed a special technique of joining stone plates together. The impressive result of this method can also be seen in the Cathedral of St James in Šibenik.

# KLAPA

The longing and melancholy of the Dalmatian soul are reflected in the a cappella songs known as klapa. Klapa is both the name of the choir and of the songs, which used to be reserved exclusively for men. Today there are also mixed and women-only choirs. The tradition of singing the songs without instrumental accompaniment has also been relaxed: guitars and tamboritzas, an instrument that resembles the mandolin, form part of many klapa performances. Good choirs develop an intense acoustic fusion that captivates every listener. The songs are about love, Dalmatia's beauty, and patriotism. Since Croatia's independence, the klapa have undergone a revival and have even found their way into Croatian pop music. When Klapa Intrade performs with pop singer Tomislav Bralić, the concerts are sold out in next to no time.

# LIGHTHOUSES

At all the important locations along the coast, on islands, in front of cliffs and shallow waters, navigational aids mark out the shipping routes both day and night. Many of the lighthouses built under Austro-Hungarian rule during the mid-19th century are now listed and stand in scenic locations. Several years ago nine of these Dalmatian lighthouses, which are now operated automatically, were converted to apartments that are rented out to holidaymakers. To name a few: one stands at the harbour entrance of Makarska, two others on the islands of Dugi otok and Lastovo as well as others far out at sea, on Sušak and Palagruža. *Information: Croatian National Tourist Board (tel. 069 238 53 50), further information also available at www.lighthouses-croatia.com*

# MARINE LIFE

The flora and fauna in the sea off the Croatian coast are largely intact because of the very good water quality. Many molluscs, sponges, crabs, lobsters, squid and cuttlefish live in the habitat provided by the rugged underwater rocks. Some of the species that are fished are common dentex, mullet, temperate bass, European anchovy and mackerel. The eastern Adriatic is still home to around 360 different species of fish.

Dolphins are sighted regularly off the Croatian coast. The environmental organization Blue World recorded a high concentration of dolphins around the island of Vis, where it wants to launch studies to research and protect these marine mammals *(www.blue-world. org)*.

Tourism, however, poses a threat to the rich fish populations, because the increasing demand frequently leads to overfishing. As a result there are hardly any sizable tuna swarms left in the eastern Adriatic. This has caused the Croats to switch to fish farming. This aquaculture produces around 10,000 tons of fish every year, supplying not only the country's restaurants, but also, and mostly, destined for export.

# NATURE CONSERVATION

Large tracts of the coastline seem to have been left untouched and undeveloped, yet this first impression is a false one, because wherever the state hoped for profits from tourism, construction took place with little regard for the environment, both during the Yugoslav era and after Croatian independence, making the rugged coast into a tourist-friendly concrete landscape and leaving all sewage removal to the sea.

This has changed with increasing environmental awareness. Channelling sewage into a drainage system is a problem that is now being addressed firmly, in the Split/Kaštelanska Riviera, where the harbour and the industry had had a serious negative impact on the water quality. Since 2007 the state-run Coast Project has had International help in its efforts to centralize the environmental efforts along the entire Dalmatian coastline and to increase the population's understanding for these measures. Conservation is also being promoted in Dalmatia's five national parks and the many nature reserves.

## WATER QUALITY

Croatia is a watery paradise. Internationally conducted and recognized tests constantly prove the high water quality of the Croatian Adriatic, which is one of the cleanest bodies of waters in the Mediterranean. There are a total of 116 Blue Flag beaches, but only around 29 of them are in Dalmatia, which does not necessary suggest a worse water quality, but rather that the local authorities are lukewarm (information under *www.blueflag.org*). Unless in the vicinity of the larger ports, you needn't worry about the cleanliness of the water.

## WINDS

The weather on the Adriatic is determined by wind. The Jugo or the Sirocco bring moist, muggy air masses from the south. It can show up at any

time of year. The Mistral, which blows in from the sea from the late afternoon to

Despite the sunshine, fishing is a tough way to earn a living

the early evening, is a welcome refreshment in the summer months for visitors and locals alike. The Bora on the other hand is the dreaded icy katabatic wind from the northeast; it opens up the sky for sunny weather, but makes the sea dangerously choppy in the process. Individual gusts can reach top speeds of up to 200 kph.

# FOOD & DRINK

**Wafer-thin Dalmatian prosciutto, yellow sheep's cheese and salted anchovies, plus a few black olives, home-made white bread, salad and sun-ripened tomatoes along with home-made wine, thinned with water: these typical treats are a good place to start a culinary exploration of Dalmatia.**

The simple, tasty dishes have a pleasant salty flavour and are prepared without lots of fat, making them light, healthy fare ideal for the hot summer months. Hotel guests booking full board are usually offered international cuisine as well as an international breakfast. Those wishing to discover traditional Dalmatian dishes should opt for half-board or bed and breakfast and then enjoy the offerings of the local restaurants and rustic guesthouses, the *konobas*.

The Dalmatians, like most southern Europeans, aren't big on breakfast. They are happy with a cup of coffee to accompany their morning chat in a café bar *(kavana)* on their way to work. It is not until the *marenda*, the second breakfast, served in late morning, that the locals eat a more hearty meal: cold roast meat, marinated anchovies, olives, cheese, small hot dishes and wine, diluted to make *bevanda* by adding the same amount of tap water. Right up until dinner in the evening, the day's main meal, the Dalmatians use every opportunity to enjoy a *kava* (espresso).

Café bars have shot up everywhere in recent years. For the general public, they

**Pršut, olives, wine: Dalmatian delights are authentic and prepared with a lot of love and verve**

are a just about affordable alternative to the local restaurants, which have become extremely expensive by Dalmatian standards. Popular holiday destinations will also have plenty of pizzerias, tavernas and konobas.

Even though the grilled mince rolls known as *čevapčići* and the pork kebabs known as *ražnjići* are not exactly traditional Dalmatian cuisine, they are on the menus of most of the restaurants. Served with spicy *ajvar*, this speciality from Bosnia is not just tasty, it is also an inexpen-

sive alternative to fish. Fish dishes are always more expensive than meat dishes. The prices charged in Dalmatia's restaurants are only slightly cheaper than those in western Europe.

Fish and seafood dishes are the local speciality. They are prepared in many different ways: as salads, in black calamari risotto, on spaghetti or homemade ribbon-style pasta. If you would like to order scampi, bear in mind they are usually served in their shell. Practise de-shelling them with grilled scampi first, then work

# LOCAL SPECIALITIES

▶ **Ajvar** – spicy paste made of peppers and tomatoes, served with grilled meat

▶ **Brodet od riba** – fish stew: different types of fish in a sauce made of olive oil, wine, onions, garlic and parsley

▶ **Dalmatinski pršut** – mildly smoked Dalmatian prosciutto

▶ **Djuveč** – side dish served with grilled meat dishes, made of rice and tomatoes, peppers and onions; served with meat it forms a main dish

▶ **Fritule** – deep-fried yeast dough, dusted with icing sugar

▶ **Koštradina** – stewed lamb, often served with Dalmatian tomato sauce

▶ **Lozovaca und Travarica** – Dalmatian grape and herb schnapps specialities, can also be obtained as ointments to treat rheumatism (photo right)

▶ **Mantala** – sweet grape-must bread, a speciality from southern Dalmatia

▶ **Mixed Grill** – various small grilled beef, pork and lamb steaks served with *ajvar*

▶ **Palačinke** – pancakes with a jam or chocolate sauce

▶ **Paški sir** – the sheep's cheese from the island of Pag is a spicy appetizer (photo left)

▶ **Pašticada** – marinated beef wrapped in bacon and prepared in red wine

▶ **Pljeskavica** – grilled minced steak

▶ **Risotto** – rice cooked in its sauce with side dishes such as shellfish, scampi and squid

▶ **Rožata** – vanilla mousse made of eggs and milk covered in caramel

▶ **Salata od hobotnice** – squid salad in a spicy olive oil marinade

▶ **Slane srdelje** – salted anchovies

▶ **Vitalac** – Dalmatian haggis: lamb offal, stuffed in intestines and grilled

your way up to poached *skampi buzara*, in a tasty sauce of wine, tomatoes and different vegetables.

Gilt-head bream *(lavrata)*, temperate bass *(brancin)*, dried cod *(bakalar)* and tuna *(tuna)* can be found on most menus. Fish prepared in a salt crust *(riba u soli)* is particularly delicious. Dried cod *(bakalar)* is a speciality, either served with white sauce and potatoes or as a mousse.

The kilo price listed on the menus always causes confusion among tourists. This price obviously does not mean that you have to order 1 kg of fish. You will be charged for the weight of your portion, approx. 250 g. The small, incredibly tasty sardines, fresh from the grill, marinated, or pickled in salt, are considered poor man's fare, which is why they can only be found on the menus of the konobas and *gostionicas* (pubs).

Beef, pork and lamb steaks are traditionally cooked on a grill over an open charcoal fire in Dalmatia. The konobas of central and southern Dalmatia serve another speciality: fish or meat, preferably lamb, is cooked gently with potatoes and vegetables under a metal bell, the *peka*, which is covered in red-hot hot charcoal. This method preserves all the flavours. Cooking times are around two hours, which is why this dish should always be ordered in advance.

The selection of side dishes is small. Common ones include boiled potatoes and chard seasoned with plenty of garlic, or djuveč rice. Chips are also on every menu. The people of Dalmatia prefer to eat white bread with their fish and meat. Most restaurants do not serve purely vegetarian dishes. However, more and more vegetarian restaurants and snack bars are opening in Dalmatia.

Wine, whether red or white, is part of every meal. Farmers make it themselves for their own consumption. This very characteristic, pleasant and inexpensive table wine, *stolno vino*, is a must, even though it will not be the same standard as a high quality wine. This wine is also obtainable in 0.7 litre bottles, labelled with its place of origin. The best-known red wines are probably *Dingač* and *Postup* from the Pelješac peninsula. They

Croatia's best red wines come from Pelješac peninsula

were delivered to the Viennese court as 'imperial wines' during the days of the Austro-Hungarian monarchy. *Grk*, a white wine from Lumbarda on the island of Korčula, enjoys a particularly good reputation.

Recently, young winegrowers from all over Croatia have been competing to turn their own grapes into quality wines. All of these dry wines have a high alcohol content of more than 12 percent. The front runner, though, is the sweet dessert wine *prošek*, which has an alcohol content of more than 16 percent. Beer lovers will be happy to know that Dalmatia has several breweries and lager can be bought everywhere.

# SHOPPING

Unusual souvenirs are unfortunately uncommon in Dalmatia. The souvenirs available here are typical of tourist destinations, including jewellery, wood carvings and embroidered doilies, ties, fountain pens and biros. The only reason they make for original souvenirs is that they were invented here in Croatia. That is why your best bet is 'back to nature', because the regional products are unrivalled!

## ART

Many artists live and work in Dalmatia. One of them is Ive Kora on Brač, whose sculptures carved out of olive wood have an incredibly sensuous feel. With a bit of luck you will be able to find a gallery with works by local artists in almost every Dalmatian town.

## HONEY

Dalmatian herbs and scented maquis produce the perfect conditions for lots of differently flavoured honeys. The island of Hvar has lavender-flavoured honey. Honey, like oil, is sold at markets and at the side of the road by the producers.

## LACE DOILIES & FILIGREE JEWELLERY

The island of Pag is famous for its fine lace, produced by the women with a lot of hard work at home. Many sell their lace doilies and napkins at the market or outside the island's lace museum, and at handsome prices too. Filigree jewellery also has a long tradition in Dalmatia and was probably taken over from the Ottomans. Most of the silver and gold items available today are not of particularly good quality. Since they are sold at relatively inexpensive prices, they still make for a nice, 'local' souvenir.

## LAVENDER

When the lavender fields are in bloom on Hvar, then the entire island is immersed in the scent of this moth-repellent herb. Lavender can be bought in a small pouch or in bulk, as an oil or as a soap or bath product.

## MUSIC

You will see: as soon as you have heard one of the mournful polyphonic Dalma-

## Fleur de sel, award-winning olive oil, fancy schnapps – culinary souvenirs are always popular

tian songs, this gentle, melancholy music will not let you go anymore. A CD of one of the famous *klapa* choirs will let you take a bit of the Dalmatian attitude towards life home with you.

### OLIVE OIL

Producers often sell their cold-pressed oil by the side of the road or at the market. Sometimes they refine it with herbs such as rosemary or by adding garlic to it. Tourist information centres will be able to tell you where you can get truly pure oil. It is also available in supermarkets. The brand 'Zvijezda' has a particularly good reputation!

### SALT

Sea salt has been obtained in Dalmatia through the process of evaporation since time immemorial. It is a pure and healthy natural product. More than 75 minerals were found in the salt obtained from the salt pans of Pag. Coarse and fine sea salt as well as 'fleur de sel', 'flower of salt', is available in supermarkets or from the salt pans direct.

### WINE & SCHNAPPS

The red wines of the Pelješac peninsula are available in every supermarket. It is, of course, much more fun to taste them at the vineyard and choose them there. Along Pelješac's wine route there are several establishments offering tastings.

When it comes to schnapps, it is best to beware of home brews. Although it is offered as a particular speciality, it is often of lesser quality. The grappa-like *lozovaca*, the aromatic *travarica* (herbal schnapps) or the rare *rogač*, obtained from the fruits of the carob tree, should be bought from specialist suppliers or from a well-known producer.

# THE PERFECT ROUTE

## MEDITERRANEAN ARCHITECTURE & WAY OF LIFE

The route begins in the lively city of ① *Zadar* → p. 46. Following the Adria Magistrale E65 southeastwards, make your way past the bare silhouettes of the islands of Ugljan and Pašman until you reach ② *Biograd na Moru* → p. 34, the heart of the Biograd Riviera, where glorious beaches are the perfect spot for a dip in the ocean.

## ART & NATURE FROM ŠIBENIK TO TROGIR

Experience the stone remains of Dalmatian Renaissance architecture in ③ *Šibenik* → p. 38. A few kilometres away the Krka gurgles and gushes through the gorges and over the cascades of Krka National Park. Filigree stonemasonry of the highest quality adorns the Romanesque portal of ④ *Trogir Cathedral* → p. 74.

## MINI CASTLES & LAVISH VEGETATION

Doll's house-like fortresses line the Kaštelanska Riviera all the way to ⑤ *Split* → p. 68, where the hustle and bustle of a port with its museums, shops, cafés and restaurants has invaded the walls of the Roman imperial palace. A fun and (most likely) wet rafting adventure awaits in ⑥ *Omiš* → p. 67 in Cetina Gorge.

## GORGEOUS BEACH & QUEEN OF THE ADRIATIC

The ⑦ *Makarska Riviera* → p. 65 boasts the gorgeous beach of Punta Rata. After that there is a somewhat longer stretch to Dalmatia's finest gem, ⑧ *Dubrovnik* → p. 81 (photo left). A wonderfully preserved old town featuring Gothic and Renaissance architecture, international flair and outstanding restaurants as well as the idyllic bays of the offshore island of Lokrum will stimulate all of your senses.

## VILLAS & FRESH OYSTERS

One tip, if you have some time, is to take a boat trip to the Elephiti Islands of Lopud and Šipan, where Dubrovnik's nobility had their summer villas. Just how the notable inhabitants of majestic Dubrovnik lived is demonstrated by Trsteno Arboretum (photo right), a manor house with a lavish garden laid out in the 16th century. The route continues northwards to ⑨ *Ston* → p. 97, where you simply must try the fresh oysters!

# Experience the diverse facets of Dalmatia, along the Croatian coast with detours to the offshore islands

## WINE TASTING & ISLAND-HOPPING

The best growers of Dingač , the local red wine, can be found on ⑩ *Pelješac Peninsula* → p. 95. The sea is once again the attraction of the small town of Orebič. This is the place to start island-hopping, the first trip being just a short one from Orebič to ⑪ *Korčula* → p. 90 on the island of the same name; this atmosheric little town has a magical Mediterranean quality.

## LIFESTYLE, LAVENDER & SANDY BAYS

Return to the mainland via Pelješac and travel northwards. Around ⑫ *Drvenik* → p. 65 is another good island detour, to Dalmatia's fanciest island, ⑬ *Hvar* → p. 60, but this excursion will require an extra two days. Taking the narrow, winding road across Hvar from east to west, you will drive by fragrant lavender fields, pretty sandy bays and remote villages before reaching the fashionable town of Hvar.

## GOLDEN CAPE, RURAL IDYLL & BUZZING LIFE

Further along the coast, it is a somewhat longer boat trip to Sumarin on the island of ⑭ *Brač* → p. 54 and Croatia's most famous beach, the Golden Cape near Bol. Pučišća and Škrip on the north coast are the places to enjoy Brač's quieter attractions, before soaking up the island atmosphere one last time in the lively main town of ⑮ *Supetar* → p. 58. Then the ferry will take you back to the mainland and to Split.

Approx. 500 mi. Actual driving time 24–36 hrs. Detailed map of the route on the back cover, in the road atlas and the pull-out map.

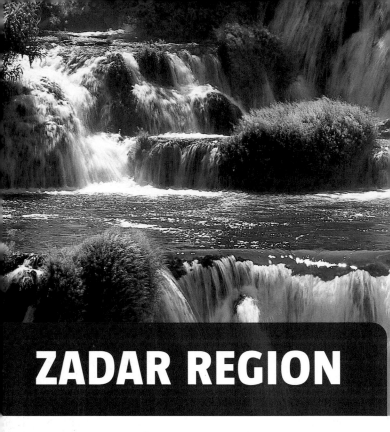

# ZADAR REGION

**The cities of Zadar and Šibenik, with their splendour of art-historical treasures, are the major towns of Dalmatia's two northernmost government districts, in which the diversity and beauty of this coastline so rich in bays and islands come together.**

Along the northern section of the mainland, the Velebit mountains, which are characterized by steep, bare, ochre rocks on their seaward side, reach all the way to the Adriatic. Here the Velika Paklenica and the Mala Paklenica bubble and flow along to the sea, through wide, imposing gorges. They form the heart of Paklenica National Park.

The Krka has cut its channel through the inhospitable, sparsely populated Zagora, the rocky, arid karst plateau in the hinterland. In the narrow valley through which the waters of the Krka find their way, the flora and fauna flourish in lavish diversity. There are countless islets and reefs off the coast of the mainland. In the north there are the elongated islands of Ugljan, Pašman and Dugi otok, off Šibenik is the Kornati archipelago, mainly uninhabited islets of whitish-grey rock surrounded by the azure-blue Adriatic. From May to September the attractive waters of Šibenik are filled with sailboats and motorboats from all over Europe. The twelve marinas of the former fishing towns along the coast can accommodate well over 3000 boats. The lower Krka, like the Kornati archipelago, is a designated national

Photo: Krka cascades

Musical waves and history set in stone: northern Dalmatia combines unique natural and artistic treasures

park. Both are described in the chapter 'Trips & tours'.

# BIOGRAD RIVIERA

**(131 D5)** *(ɯ F–G4)* **The peaks of Pašman island protect the forested mainland coast along the Pašmanski Kanal from strong winds coming in from the open sea.**

In addition, the Biograd Riviera, with places such as *Biograd na moru, Sv. Filip i Jakov* and *Pakoštane,* is considered a great base for sailing excursions to the Kornati archipelago.

Among the gentle hills of the *Ravni Kotari* region in the hinterland, the turquoise Lake Vrana *(Vransko jezero)* makes for an interesting visual contrast to the azure of the Adriatic with its Mediterranean vegetation. Birdwatchers and anglers will also be able to pursue their interests here.

Biograd: enjoy a relaxing end to the day in the cafés along the waterfront promenade

## TOWNS ALONG THE BIOGRAD RIVIERA

**BIOGRAD NA MORU** (131 D5) *(𝄞 F4)*
This small town (population: 6000) with its two marinas (950 moorings) is particularly popular with sailors. Every night they can be heard recounting their sailors' yarns in bars, taverns and restaurants. This town also has plenty to offer those on a beach holiday. The konoba *Vapor (Obala Kralja Petra Krešimira IV | tel. 023 38 54 82 | Moderate)* on the waterfront is a wonderfully idyllic spot to enjoy some pršut (dry-cured ham), grilled salmon and wine. Every now and then the owners go out fishing themselves, after which they are particularly proud to present their catch. The tiny konoba Barba *(Frankopanska 2 | tel. 023 38 44 51 | Budget)* is a cosy establishment, where you may find yourself singing Dalmatian folk songs over your grilled fish and tangy wine.

Night owls meet in the cafés along the Riva waterfront promenade. Lavender Bed Bar in the Hotel Adriatic, with its comfortable lounge chairs and lavender scent, is the absolute front-runner among the party crowd. From the recently updated 1970s hotels *Kornati (102 rooms | tel. 023 35 83 33 | Moderate)* and *Ilirija (166 rooms | tel. 023 39 65 55 | www.ilirijabiograd.com | Moderate)*, it is just a stone's throw to the pebble beach, to the town centre and to the waterfront with its attractive flower beds and palm trees. The accommodation at *Villa Maimare (17 rooms | Marka Marulića 1 | tel. 023 38 43 58 | www. maimare.hr | Budget)* is both more individual and less expensive and it is close to the town centre and the beach to boot. Walking along this promenade, you will come across the *Regional Museum*, which houses a sensational discovery: the cargo of a trading ship that sank in the Pašmanski Kanal when sailing from Venice to Constantinople in the 16th century. Leather-framed spectacles, shaving knives, sewing needles, men's shirts and woolly hats: the collection of everyday items from this era is considered one of the most extensive in the world (*summer Mon–Sat 9am–noon, 6pm–11pm | on the promenade | 12 kunas*).

There is a car ferry that makes its way from Biograd to Tkon/Pašman up to eight times a day. Information: *Tourist Info | Trg hrvatskih velikana 2 | Biograd na moru | tel. 023 38 31 23 | www.tzg biograd.hr*

## PAKOŠTANE (131 D5) (*📖 G4*)

This coastal village (population: 1800), surrounded by pine woods, is situated between the sea and Lake Vrana. The old core with its winding alleys, tiny squares and narrow courtyards still looks like a real ancient Dalmatian fishing village. It is surrounded by many new houses with well-tended gardens. One original accommodation option that will appeal both to sports enthusiasts and families is provided by the Polynesian-style straw huts of *Club Pakoštane (455 huts | Brune Busica 45 | tel. 023 25 30 60 | www. club pakostane.hr | Budget)*. The all-in complex is situated on a hillside above an attractive pebble beach and offers a wide array of sporting and entertainment activities. One popular eatery is the restaurant *Tri Ferala* with eels and frogs from Lake Vrana *(Ivana Meštrovića 9 | tel. 023 38 11 07 | www.tri-ferala.biz | Moderate)*.

You can sail from Pakoštane to the small and still quite unspoilt island of *Vrgada*. Private accommodation available. *Information: Tourist Info | Pakoštane | tel. 023 38 18 92 | www.pakostane.hr*

## SV. FILIP I JAKOV (131 D5) (*📖 F4*)

Tranquil and familiar are two adjectives that characterize this pleasant little town (population: 1500). It has shallow pebble beaches and you can take a taxi boat to the uninhabited and barely fre-

quented bathing island of *Babac*. 1.5 km (0.9 mi) further inland is the church Sv. Roko (11th century), which stands in a picturesque setting alone in a field. This church is the last reminder of the great medieval Benedictine abbey of Rogovo. Its monks founded Sv. Filip i Jakov as their supply port. Every year on 16 August the **INSIDERTIP** Sv. Roko festival is celebrated around the church. Accommodation can be found in the basic seaside campsite of *Dardin (520 pitches | tel. 023 38 86 07)*. *Information: Tourist Info | Kuntrata | Sveti Filip i Jakov | tel. 023 38 90 71 | www.sv-filipjakov.hr*

## VRANA AND LAKE VRANA (VRANSKO JEZERO) (131 D5) (*📖 F5*)

Leaving the town that is home to the remains of Vrana Castle and the *Maškovica*

---

## MARCO POLO HIGHLIGHTS

⭐ **Panoramic Road**
Island road on Dugi otok with wonderful views → p. 36

⭐ **Telašćica Nature Park**
The sea penetrates deep into the bizarre karst landscape → p. 38

⭐ **Šibenik's old town**
Historic listed buildings → p. 39

⭐ **Cathedral of Saint James**
Busts and tunnel vaults in Šibenik → p. 39

⭐ **Primošten**
This island village is known for its top-quality wines → p. 42

⭐ **Zadar's Old Town**
Mediterranean life in a cultural and historical treasure trove → p. 47

*Han* caravanserai, a rare example of Ottoman architecture in Dalmatia, the road winds its way towards Benkovac, from the plain to the plateau. ⚜ From the edge of the latter you will have far-reaching views of the turquoise-green *Vransko jezero*, framed by a ring of reeds. It has been a nature park since 1999 *(20 kunas | www. vransko-jezero.hr)*. The fish-rich freshwater lake, which is a good 10 km (6.2 mi) long and up to 4 km (2.5 mi) wide, is home to eels, pike, carp and catfish.

☺ The northwest shores are an ornithological reserve. The wide reed belt is home to more than 240 bird species, including pygmy cormorants, western marsh harriers, acrocephalus warblers, purple herons, little egrets and great egrets. A one-day fishing licence (70 kunas) as well as fishing equipment are available from the *Ckrvine* campsite *(tel. 023 63 61 93)* on the north shore. Those not wishing to trust their own fishing skills will find fish from Lake Vrana on the menu of the rustic *Vransko Jezero* restaurant *(tel. 023 63 61 93 | Budget)*. The view from ⚜ ● Kamenjak hill (sign reads Vidikovac) of the lake, the coastline and the Kornati islands surrounded by the blue of the sea is fantastic.

# DUGI OTOK

(130 B–C4–5) *(ᗪ D–F 3–4)* **Dugi otok (population: 2400), Croatia's 'Long Island', is located on the fringe of the north Dalmatian archipelago.**
From the northern to the southern tip it measures 52 km (32 mi) and has a width of 1 to 4 km (2.5 mi). The island's north is forested and green, while the south, which is also home to the island's largest town of *Sali* (population: 600) and ● *Telašćica Nature Park*, has a karst landscape, similar to the small islands of the neighbouring Kornati Islands National Park.

⚜ There is a well-surfaced road leaving Sali that connects all 14 of the island's villages and hamlets, before reaching the village of *Božava* all the way in the north of Dugi otok. This ★ *panoramic road* alone is reason enough to take the car over from the mainland, even just for a day trip, as it affords fabulous views of the islands between the mainland and Dugi otok and of the Adriatic. ☺ One appealing and also more environmentally friendly alternative is to mountain bike this route and take some detours along dirt tracks to remote villages. A special

# UNDER FULL SAIL

They once brought olives, wine and salt all the way to Trieste and Venice. Today the small motor-assisted sailboats show tourists the Dalmatian island world at its most beautiful. They anchor in bays that are inaccessible from the land, and they stop in picturesque towns whose most magnificent side can only be fully appreciated from the water. Every one of these family-owned wooden boats is different; some of them are based on new models, some on traditional ones. The cabins on board, rarely more than a dozen, do not have the space for anything but the necessities. The sun deck is all the larger. In the tiny galley Dalmatian home-cooked fare is prepared for all the guests. There are various operators, e.g. in UK *Sail Croatia Adventure| Tel. 0845 257 82 89 | www.sail-croatia.com*

bike map is available from Zadar's tourist board.

The dreamy villages look quite magical from afar. But in those places that rarely see holidaymakers, many houses are empty or else inhabited almost only by old people. Their children usually live all over the world.

Tourism on Dugi otok (124 sq km, (48 sq mi) is nowhere near as developed as on the other Dalmatian islands of this size. That is its great appeal for everyone seeking personal encounters with fishermen and farmers and for nature lovers, with trails leading to remote beaches. For that reason it is not surprising that Dugi otok is so popular with travellers, sailors and divers who spurn the blandishments of the tour operators.

## PLACES ON DUGI OTOK

**BOŽAVA** (130 B4) (*ₐD3*)

This small, picturesque village (population: 160), situated in a sheltered harbour bay, is Dugi otok's tourist centre, because just a few minutes' walk away is the island's largest hotel complex, which has been refurbished to very modern standards. It lies hidden in a dense pine forest *(Hotels Božava | 103 rooms, 18 apartments. | tel. 023 29 12 91 | www. hoteli-bozava.hr | Moderate–Expensive)*. From here you will have the best view of the bay in which sailing yachts moor in the evenings. It is possible to book a diving excursion with guides in *Božava (tel. 023 31 88 91 | www.bozava.de)* diving school.

3 km (1.9 mi) away is the natural, shallow **INSIDER TIP** bay of *Sakarun* with its sandy beach. It is an ideal place to go swimming and play around, especially for little children. You will, however, have to bring your own sunshades, sunloungers and provisions.

Great for diving: the steep coastline of Dugio

At the end of the road the 45 m *Veli rat lighthouse* has stood on the northwestern tip of Dugi otok since 1849, surrounded by pine forests and good bathing spots. **INSIDER TIP** There are two apartments in the lighthouse that are let out to holidaymakers. *Information: www. lighthouses-croatia.com and Croatian National Tourist Board (see 'Travel tips')*

Opposite, in the fishing village of *Verunic*, you will find accommodation in a more familiar setting right on the waterfront in the *Gorgonia Apartments (3 apartments | tel. 023 37 81 53 | www.gorgonia. hr | Budget)*.

### SALI (130 C5) (*ᴍ E4*)

Dugi otok's economic and administrative centre, Sali, gets its name from the salt mines from which the precious sea salt was once obtained. The island's largest settlement has maintained its fishing tradition for more than a thousand years. This is confirmed by a document from around 990 AD. The Gothic parish church of *Sv. Marija* was built there in the 15th century, on the site of a small, early medieval church. Remains of the Croatian-wattle ornamentation and the large wooden altar have survived (only open during services). Sali traditionally celebrates INSIDER TIP *Salijske užanske*, its village festival in early August, with a donkey race.

Holidaymakers, boating visitors and divers all like to use Sali as a starting point for tours to Telašćica Nature Park and to the Kornati archipelago. The village has three diving schools that run excursions to the Kornati. *Hotel Sali*, built on a slight elevation above the sea, is a good five minutes from the centre (*52 rooms | tel. 023 37 70 49 | www.hotel-sali.hr | Moderate*). The locals like to come to the konoba *Kod Sipe (Sali 174 | tel. 023 37 71 37 | Budget–Moderate*) to play cards. Fish and seafood are prepared simply, but always in a tasty manner.

### TELAŠĆICA-NATURE PARK ★
(130 C5) (*ᴍ E4*)

The nature park with its approx. 8 km (5 mi) bay of ● Telašćica at the end of the island is well worth a visit. Telašćica possesses the safest and largest natural harbour of the Adriatic, set against a magnificent backdrop of steep, rugged and rocky mountains. On the west coast the 146m *Kliff Grpašćak* rises spectacularly from the sea. It is easy to reach via a path from Mir Bay, where excursion boats also call in. The water in the salt-water lake just five minutes' walk away is always 6 degrees warmer than the sea. If you announce your arrival in good time, the tavern Go Ro in Magrovica Bay (*tel. 098 85 35 34 | Moderate*) will serve you a delicious lamb dish, prepared under a peka. *National park 60 kunas for one day | www.telascica.hr*

## BOAT CONNECTIONS

You can take the car ferry from *Zadar* to *Brbinj;* there are also daily hydrofoil departures from *Zadar* to *Sali. Information at www.jadrolinija.hr*

## INFORMATION

**TOURIST INFO**
*Sali | tel. 023 37 70 94 | www.dugiotok.hr*

# ŠIBENIK

(132 B2) (*ᴍ F–G5*)   **Before the Krka pushes its water through 5 km (3.1 mi) of narrow canal-like gorge into the sea, it spreads out one last time into a lake.** In this naturally sheltered nook, the immigrant Croats built their 9th century fortress in the same spot that had seen an Illyrian castle in earlier times. It was not long before seafarers and pirates, fishermen and farmers settled at the foot of the 70 m (77 yd) karst rock. Modern-day Šibenik (population: 40,000) has grown from this initial core. Since 2000 the Cathedral of St James has been on the list of Unesco World Heritage Sites. The cascades of the Krka north of the town are a beautiful addition to one of Croatia's most attractive national parks (*see 'Trips & tours'*). Šibenik's tourist area is located on the seafront 6 km (3.7 mi) from the centre.

## SIGHTSEEING

### OLD TOWN ★

From the waterfront promenade there is a set of stairs leading through the Sea Gate up to *Trg Republike Hrvatske* alleys that lead up to the ruined fortress of Sv. Mihovil (Saint Michael). This is a ↘↙ path worth taking, as it affords wide-ranging views over the crowded red-tiled roofs and the green valley of the Krka.

From the fortress of Sv. Mihovil you get the best views of Šibenik

(Square of the Republic of Croatia) on which stands the Cathedral of *St James*. The *Prince's Palace* (14–16th centuries) next to the basilica, which houses several ancient treasures, is now used as a city museum *(summer, daily 10am–1pm, 6pm–9pm | 12 kunas)*. Opposite it, the town hall is housed in the two-storey city loggia, whose façade has a lovely row of round arches. The loggia was completely destroyed during World War II and later rebuilt in its original style.

Take the stairs to its left to get to the attractive Foscolo Palace (15th century), whose façade is adorned by late-Gothic windows. There are many similarly beautiful palaces hidden in the winding

### CATHEDRAL OF SAINT JAMES ★

This magnificent building had a long construction period (1431–1555), which explains the mix of stylistic elements from Gothic and Renaissance. The roof structure is unique for this period: a barrel vault of self-supporting stone slabs over the nave, the aisles, the apses and the dome. Around the apses' outer wall, at the viewer's eye level, there is a frieze with more than 70 stone portraits: citizens, farmers, fishermen, high-standing men, women, children, all contemporaries of the great architect and sculptor Juraj Dalmatinac (born early 15th century, died in Šibenik in 1473). The artistically designed baptistery is also largely attrib-

# ŠIBENIK

uted to him. *April–Sept 8.30am–8pm, Oct–Mar 8.30am–noon, 4pm–6.30pm | 10 kunas*

Outside the main portal is the *Dalmatinac Monument*, created by Croatia's probably most famous sculptor of the 20th century, Ivan Meštrović.

## FOOD & DRINK

In the streets of the old town there are a number of bars and cafés. In the summertime there are often only a few free spaces.

### GRADSKA VIJEĆNICA

Šibenik's terrace with the most romantic backdrop: the restaurant in the loggia arcade does not just impress with its flair, it also serves sophisticated and always fresh fish dishes. *Trg Republike Hrvatske 3 | tel. 022 2136 05 | Moderate*

▶ **PELEGRINI**

Situated above Bunari Museum and decorated in a rustic, minimalist style, this konoba is the culinary meeting place in Šibenik, serving sophisticated cuisine from traditional to sushi. *Jurja Dalmatinca 1 | tel. 022 2137 01 | Expensive*

### TINEL

Simpler dishes such as *pašticada* and goulash for smaller wallets, as well as good (and more expensive) fish and seafood. *Trg Pučkih Kapetana | tel. 023 3318 15 | Budget–Moderate*

## BEACHES

There is no place to go swimming right in the town. There is a nice pebble beach on *Zablaće peninsula* around the Solaris hotel complex 6 km (3.7 mi) away and in Vodice 10 km (6.2 mi) away, where peop-

Cathedral of St. James in Šibenik: the self-supporting tunnel vault is considered a structural feat

le meet at the highly praised *Plava Plaža* (pebbles, rocks, concrete).

## ENTERTAINMENT

When the Šibenik-born DJ Sasha Gardijan puts on his show in *Cohiba*, it is a techno spectacular *(Stube Petra Kaera | old town)*. *No 4 Club* is a mix between bar, lounge and restaurant, where live bands also perform from time to time *(trg Dinka Zavorovica 4)*.

## WHERE TO STAY

### SOLARIS HOLIDAY RESORT

The expansive holiday complex on a green peninsula (6 km, 3.7 mi) outside of the town centre) consists of several 3-star hotels, apartment villas and the modern Aqualand leisure pool, which also has a wellness centre (thalasso therapy, diverse massage and beauty treatments). Sporting activities such as aqua aerobics, tennis, football and a fitness trail mean that active spirits have plenty to entertain them too. *1300 rooms | Hotelsko naselje Solaris | tel. 022 36 10 01 | www. solaris.hr | Moderate*

## BOAT CONNECTIONS

A foot-passenger ferry departs from *Šibenik* and *Vodice* up to five times a day for *Zlarin* and *Prvić;* from *Šibenik* up to three times a day for *Kaprije* and *Žirje* and from *Brodarica* several times a day for *Krapanj*.

## INFORMATION

### TOURIST INFO

*Obala Dr. Franje Tuđmana 5 | tel. 022 21 44 11 | www.sibenik-tourism.hr*

## WHERE TO GO

### BRODARICA (132 B2) (*Ø G5*)

The townspeople like to come to this small town 6 km (3.7 mi) south of Šibenik, opposite the island of Krapanj, for dinner. The *Zlatna ribica* restaurant is popular for its fish stew *(brodet),* served Dalmatian-style with *polenta (Krapanjskih spužvara 46 | tel. 022 35 06 95 | Moderate)*. It is connected to a lovingly run family guesthouse. In addition to the modern rooms in the main building there are a few bungalows right by the sea (22 rooms). *Information: Tourist Info | Krapanj-Brodarica | tel. 022 35 06 12 | www.tz-brodarica.hr*

### MURTER (132 A2) (*Ø F4*)

A drawbridge in the small town of *Tisno* connects the 19 sq km (7.3 sq mi) island (population: 5000) with the mainland. Murter is a green island with fields, orchards and vineyards as well as pretty bathing bays, but without any noteworthy cultural attractions. All of the island's villages *(Murter, Betina and Jezera)* have a marina. That makes Murter an important base for sailors, who set off from here for excursions to the Kornati archipelago. In addition there are a number of holiday homes and campsites.

On the mainland side, near the town of Jezera, is the holiday resort of *Lovišća* in a pebble beach bay *(camping and 83 apartments | tel. 022 43 96 00 | www.jezera-kornati.hr)*. On the nearby shady campsite of *Slanica*, which has just 100 pitches, you can hire boats, bicycles and scooters *(Podvrsak b.b. | tel. 022 78 58 04 9 | www.murter-slanica.hr)*. The *Stomorin* hotel *in Hramina Marina* in Murter has a cool and modern design *(10 rooms | tel. 022 43 44 11 | www.marina-hramina.hr | Moderate)*. Why not enjoy some aromatically grilled fish at sunset on the terrace of *Zminjak* restaurant on

View from the mainland of the small island with the picture book village of Primošten

Murter's offshore island *(only May–Sept | Moderate)*. *Information: Tourist Info | Rudina | Murter | tel. 022 43 49 95 | www.tzo-murter.hr. 25 km (15.5 mi) west*

### PRIMOŠTEN ⭐ (132 B3) (*m* F5)

The old, picturesque part of the fishing village (population: 1500) used to be on a small island, but it is now connected to the mainland via a causeway. The nearby vineyards grow *babić*, a top quality Dalmatian wine. The village gets crowded in the summer months with many souvenir shops, taverns and café bars, because Primošten is also a popular destination for the locals.

The cosy INSIDER TIP *Taverna Dalmacija* is a good place to eat. The green pasta with seafood is delicious *(Put Murve 15 | tel. 022 57 00 09 | Moderate)*. Night owls go to Dalmatia's largest night club *Aurora (only July–Sept | 3 km (1.9 mi) inland | www.auroraclub.hr)* to have some fun. A few minutes' walk out of town is the newly renovated 4-star Zora resort, which offers a large range of activities and is beautifully situated on a forested peninsula *(327 rooms | tel. 022 57 00 48 | www.hotelzora-adriatiq.com | Moderate–Expensive)*. *Information: Tourist Info | Trg biskupa Josipa Arnerića 2 | Primošten | tel. 022 57 11 61 | www.tz-primosten.hr. 30 km (18.6 mi) to the south*

### ŠIBENIK ARCHIPELAGO
(132 A2–3) (*m* G5)

The Šibenik Archipelago *(Šibensko-Kninska Županija)* only possesses around ten island communities: of the approximately 250 islands and rocky outcrops in the archipelago, most are uninhabited. It is a fascinating place for sailors, but the islands can also be explored as part of boat trips. There are a few private individuals offering accommodation, e.g. on the islands of *Prvić, Kaprije, Žirje, Zlarin* and *Krapanj*. The main sources of income used to be sponge harvesting and coral fishing. The history of these once very successful economic activities is presented in the Franciscan priory on Krapanj *(sponge production | summer daily 10am–noon, 5pm–7pm, winter on request)* and in the local museum on Zlarin *(coral exhibition | during the summer daily 8am–8pm | 8 kunas)*.

Divers will find wonderfully **INSIDER TIP** clear, species-rich waters around Krapanj, and the comfortable *Spongiola* hotel is a perfect base for their sport, because the owner is a passionate diver himself and has even created a small diving museum in his hotel *(18 rooms, 5 apartments | Obala | Krapanj | tel. 022 34 89 00 | www.spongiola.com | Moderate–Expensive)*. The island of Prvić is a quiet, idyllic spot with rock and pebble beaches that do not see many visitors. The school house in the small town of Prvić-Luka is now a magical **INSIDER TIP** hotel called *Maestral*, whose architecture and interior combine the old and the new beautifully. The menu of the adjoining Val restaurant focuses on fresh fish and seafood *(12 rooms | tel. 022 44 83 00 | www.hotelmaestral.com | Expensive)*.

## VODICE (132 A2) (ω F4)

The former fishing village (population: 4000) is now a lively holiday resort with a pedestrianized promenade around the harbour basin. Here and in the old town there are lots of bars, restaurants and souvenir shops. The whole gamut of international favourites from pizza to tacos and tortillas as well as Dalmatian cuisine can be enjoyed in the konoba Santa Maria, while browsing for a pretty painting in the adjoining gallery *(Pamuković Kamila 9 | tel. 098 21 98 69 | Moderate)*. The colourful and diverse underwater world can be explored with Vodice dive on diving trips and courses *(Braće Ćirila i Metoda 5 | tel. 09 89 19 62 33 | www.vodice-dive.com)*. The best beaches line the forested peninsula of Punta. There's a ferry service that runs to the islands of Prvić and Zlarin and to Šibenik several times a day. For boating tourists the marina is a popular location very close to Šibenik Archipelago.

Accommodation can be found both in hotels and privately. Right on the beach is the privately-run *Hotel Kristina (20 rooms | tel. 022 44 41 73 | www.hotel-kristina.hr | Moderate)*. Another recommendable hotel is *Villa Radin (12 rooms, 1 apartment | Grgura Ninskog 10 | tel. 022 44 04 15 | www.hotel-villa.radin.hr | Moderate–Expensive)*, which has a pool and is located on Punta peninsula right on the beach. Information: *Tourist Info | Ive Čota 1 a | Vodice | tel. 022 44 38 88 | www.vodice.hr. 10 km (6.2 mi) to the west*

# LOW BUDGET

▶ The *youth hostel* in Zadar is not far away from the old town in the Ljepotica neighbourhood *(only open July/Aug | 300 beds | Obala kneza Branimira 10a | tel. 023 22 48 40 | djacki-dom@zd.htnet.hr)*.

▶ Smart, modern ambience and inexpensive, good food can be found in Zadar's new self-service restaurant *Barbakan (Budget)* in the former citadel.

# UGLJAN & PAŠMAN

(130–131 B–D4–5) *(ⓜ D–E3–4)* **For the inhabitants of Zadar, the islands of *Ugljan* and *Pašman*, 3 (1.9) to 5 km (3.1mi) away, are weekend destinations.**

The islanders commute every day by ferry (approx. 30 min) to jobs and colleges institutions in the district's administrative centre. Ugljan and Pašman were originally connected to each other, but in 1883 the narrow strait of Ždrelac was made navigable. Since 1973 a bridge has spanned the canal, reconnecting the two islands.

## PLACES ON UGLJAN

Because of its favourable connection to the mainland, Ugljan (51 sq km, 19.7 sq mi) is one of the most densely populated Dalmatian islands (population: 7000). All of the seven villages are on the island's eastern side, the side facing the mainland. The mountainous west coast is rugged and difficult to access. The north on the other hand drops down gently to the sea.

The many silvery olive trees are a striking feature of the island's vegetation. Allegedly there are more than 100,000 of them. By producing olive oil, Ugljan is continuing a tradition the island was already known for in Roman times. From late November to February the ripe olives are picked. Olive oil from Ugljan (the highest quality is cold-pressed using ancient methods) is also available on Zadar market.

### KUKLJICA (130 C5) *(ⓜ E3)*

This fishing village (population: 600) is situated in a bay in the south of Ugljan. At the northern end of the bay the basic holiday resort of *Zelena punta* was built on a forested headland *(120 rooms, 124 apartments | tel. 023 37 33 38 | www.coning-turizam.com | Budget)*. The konoba *Kod Barba Tome (tel. 023 37 33 23 | Moderate)* is a popular fish restaurant; it has an original 'boat bar'. Every year in early August this village celebrates Our Lady of the Snows, during which a statue of the Madonna is carried in a procession of small boats to the church of *Gospa od sniga* in the bay of Ždrelac.

Kukljica is proud of its marina with 300 mooring spots. Hiking trails will take you to the idyllic bathing bays of *Kunćabok*, *Mali*, *Veli Sabuša* (sandy beach) and *Jelenica* (clothing optional). *Information: Tourist Info | Kukljica | tel. 023 37 32 76 | www.kukljica.hr*

### PREKO (130 C4) *(ⓜ E3)*

Preko lies directly opposite Zadar. This is where the car ferry from the mainland docks. Café bars, restaurants and shops give this place an urbane air. Preko's

You will have spectacular views from the ruined fortress of Sv. Mihovil above Preko

town beach, Jaz, is nowhere near as attractive as the small green offshore island of *Galevac-Školjić* with its pebbly bays. There is also a Franciscan priory on the island, but it is not open to the public. Above Preko are the remains of the ⚜ *fortress of Sv. Mihovil* (13th century). The walk from Preko, which takes about an hour, is definitely worth it. Once at the top, you will have wonderful panoramic views. Further recommendable hiking and mountain biking trails on the island are described on the website of the Preko tourist board. *Information: Tourist Info | Preko | tel. 023 28 61 08 | www.preko.hr*

### UGLJAN (TOWN) (130 C4) *(🗺 E3)*
Ugljan consists of several neighbourhoods. The swimming beaches of Muline are rarely crowded and are nicely situated, because you can see a whole number of smaller and larger islands from here. Rooms and apartments in private homes are available to tourists. *Information:*

*Tourist Info | Ugljan | tel. 023 28 80 11 | www.ugljan.hr*

### PLACES ON PAŠMAN

Ugljan's somewhat larger (60 sq km, 23 sq mi), but less densely populated sister island of Pašman (population: 3100) is quite similar. Here too there are just paths and trails over the rugged island peaks to the pretty bays on the west coast, all of which lead off from the only road that connects all of the island's towns on the east coast. There is a 29 km (18 mi) ⚜ **INSIDER TIP** panoramic hiking trail along the ridge, which runs all the way from the bridge to Ugljan to Tkon. Pašman has an even more rural feel than Ugljan. The farmers supply Zadar market with the copious quantities of vegetables growing in the fields around the villages. Although there is no hotel on Pašman, there are several private guesthouses and many apartments as well as private rooms and campsites on the island. Simple former fishing huts right on the sea are available through *Val Tours (Trg hrvatskih velikana | 23210 Biograd na Moru | tel. 023 38 64 79 | www.val-tours.com).*

### KRAJ (131 D5) *(m E4)*

On the outskirts of Kraj on Pašman the Franciscan priory of *Sv. Dujma u Kraju* (14th century) stands in the midst of green fields. The Renaissance cloister, library and the Baroque paintings of saints in the refectory are all worth seeing. *Summer Mon–Fri 4pm–6pm*

### PAŠMAN (TOWN) (130 C5) *(m E4)*

Even the island's main town only has a population of 300. Private rooms with breakfast included are available through *Sobe Bobić*, situated right on the water. The owners will show interested guests around their green island personally *(4 rooms | tel. 023 26 01 11 | Budget).* Next door, in ⊙ *Lanterna restaurant*, the vegetables and salads come from the restaurant's own garden *(tel. 023 26 04 06 | Moderate). Information: Tourist Info | Pašman | tel. 023 26 01 55 | www.pasman.hr*

### TKON (131 D5) *(m E4)*

The car ferry from the mainland port of Biograd na moru docks in Tkon several times a day. Around 2 km (1.2 mi) towards the town of Pašman, there is a turning to the Benedictine monastery of ● *Sv. Kuzma i Damjan* (12th century) on Ćokovac mountain. For centuries the abbey was a school of Slavonic liturgy and Glagolitic (Old Slavonic) literature. The entrance to the Gothic church bears Glagolitic inscriptions and there are stone heads hidden in the capitals. The painted wooden crucifix above the altar dates back to the 14th century. It is an interesting image that puts love above pain. Monks explain the symbolism to the visitors. *July–Sept Mon–Sat 4pm–6pm | Entry: free (donations welcome)*

### BOAT CONNECTIONS

The car ferry from Zadar–*Preko/Ugljan* goes approximately every hour during the day, while the car ferry from *Biograd–Tkon/Pašman* goes eight times a day during the peak season.

# ZADAR

### ▧ MAP INSIDE THE ▧ BACK COVER

(130 C4) *(m E3)* **As a lively port and trading town, as the economic hub and the centre of culture and transportation and as the administrative seat of the government district, Zadar (population: 80,000) is the main city of northern Dalmatia.**

Zadar's most significant attraction, the remains of more than three thousand years of urban history, can be found on the 1 km (0.6 mi) by 500 m (547 yd) peninsula that also contains the car-free old town core. Ferries dock at its quayside. A relaxed Mediterranean attitude prevails the flair here, particularly in the evenings, when young people meet at the sea organ to listen to its gentle sounds while taking in what is allegedly the most beautiful sunset on the Adriatic, before heading to the Corso in the old town. Take time to stop

### 🏙 WHERE TO START?

From the waterfront promenade **Obala Kneza Branimira** in the new town (you will find parking here too) a footbridge will take you to the peninsula with the historic town centre. Keep going straight to get to **Narodni trg,** where you will also find the tourist information.

and take in the atmosphere marked by a changeful history and art as you stroll through the narrow alleys paved with stone slabs. Climatically speaking, Zadar is in a favourable location because the mistral, a fair-weather wind, treats the town to a refreshing breeze during hot summer days.

when the rubble of the bombed homes was removed.

By the time you reach the main shopping street, *Široka Ulica*, which runs from Trg Sv. Stošije to Narodni trg, it will be obvious that the old town of Zadar is a lively open-air museum. But beforehand it is worth taking a detour

The Lion of Saint Mark watches over Zadar: detail of the Porta Terraferma on the town wall

## SIGHTSEEING

### OLD TOWN ★

At the harbour and while crossing to the mainland you can still see the town wall dating back to the late Middle Ages. The Porta Terraferma (16th century), a work by the Venetian Michele Sanmicheli, is considered the most significant Renaissance structure in Zadar. The road through the gate leads straight up to *Zeleni trg*, which is part of the Roman Forum. The remains visible here, which include a 14m Croatian-wattle ornamented column, also known as the Pillar of Shame because miscreants were tied up here in public between the Middle Ages and 1840, were only discovered in 1946

towards the sea gate on the harbour side to the attractive Romanesque *Sv. Krševan church* (12th century). It was in this church that Ladislaus of Naples was crowned King of Hungary and Dalmatia in 1403; he then went on to sell Dalmatia to Venice for 100,000 ducats six years later.

### ARCHAEOLOGICAL MUSEUM (ARHEOLOŠKI MUZEJ)

The discoveries from the time of the Illyrians, Greeks and Romans made in and around Zadar as well as unique ancient Croatian treasures from the 8th and 9th centuries are on display in a new building on the Roman Forum. *Summer daily 9am–7pm, winter daily 9am–3pm | 12 kunas*

## GOLD AND SILVER OF ZADAR (ZLATO I SREBRO ZADRA) ●

Opposite Sv. Donat the Benedictine monastery displays its unique collection of sacred metalwork, the famous 'gold and silver of Zadar'. *Summer Mon–Sat 10am–1pm, 5pm–8pm, Sun 10am–noon, winter Mon–Sat 10am–1pm | 20 kunas*

## SEA ORGAN (MORSKE ORGULJE) ●

Nature herself composes and plays an endless symphony on the world's only sea organ. Its inventor was the architect Nicola Bašić from Zadar. With the help of musicians and organ builders he successfully implemented his marvellous idea on the Riva in 2005. Over an area of more than 70m there are 35 pipes made of polyethylene in seven sections that produce a musical performance using the power of the sea. The award-winning project has been enriched by a new attraction. Bašić designed a disc that acts as a solar collector during the day and emits a mysterious light at night. It is called 'Pozdrav suncu', Sun Salutation.

## NARODNI TRG

The People's Square has been at the heart of public life since the Renaissance. It is surrounded by buildings from several different centuries: the court used to sit in the imposing city loggia (1562). The building of the former town guard (1562) with the clock tower (1798) is now the Ethnographical Museum *(summer, Mon–Fri 8am–noon, 6pm–9pm, Sat 9am–1pm, winter Mon–Fri 9am–noon, 5pm–8pm, Sat 9am–1pm | 12 kunas)*. The town hall was built by the Italians in 1936. Opposite is the magnificent Palazzo Ghirardini-Marchi from the 15th century, which is adorned by an artistically ornamented, Gothic window.

## INSIDER TIP ▶ ROWING-BOAT FERRY

A time-saving pleasure for all those with tired feet. At the harbour entrance (by the beacon) you can have Croatia's only rowing-boat ferry take you to the tip of the old town peninsula for just 7 kunas. Six men from two families share this traditional job, allowing the ferry to operate from 6am to 10pm.

## SV. DONAT AND SV. STOŠIJA

The two-storey round church of *Sv. Donat* was probably built in the early 9th century on the foundations of the forum. Ancient columns and stone fragments were used for the church walls *(summer daily 9am–10pm, winter viewing after asking the Archaeological Museum | 6 kunas)*.

Sv. Donat is connected to the Romanesque Cathedral of St Anastasia (*Sv. Stošija, 12th/13th centuries)*. The cathedral's entrance is impressively decorated with rich stonemasonry (acanthus leaves and the heads of the Apostles). Inside, a

Gothic retable dating from 1332 adorns a plain 9th-century altar. In the cathedral's left apse you will find the sarcophagus of St Anastasia *(daily 8am–6pm)*. 179 steps lead up to the  bell tower, from where you will have wonderful views of Zadar *(April–Oct daily 9.30am–1pm, 5pm–8pm | 10 kunas)*.

## SV. ŠIMUN

A few steps further towards the land gate is the Baroque church of *Sv. Šimun*. The remains of Saint Simon are kept above the main altar in an artistically decorated 14th-century sarcophagus made of more than 300kg of gold and silver.

## PEOPLE'S MUSEUM (NARODNI MUZEJ)

In addition to the local museum the museum complex in Poljana Pape Aleksandra III possesses an ethnological and a scientific department as well as an art gallery. *Summer Mon–Fri 9am–noon, 5pm–8pm, Sat 9am–1pm, winter Thu–Tue 9am–2pm, Wed 9am–noon, 5pm–9pm | 12 kunas*

## FOOD & DRINK

### FOŠA

Below the land gate at the old harbour, Foša, the quietly situated terrace of this elegant fish restaurant affords views of the sea. It is considered Zadar's best gourmet restaurant. *Daily from noon | Kralja Dmitra Zvonimira 2 | tel. 023 31 44 21 | Expensive*

### KORNAT

The restaurant at the harbour is for those who like fine dining, excellent fish dishes and outstanding wines. *Liburnska obala 6 | tel. 023 25 45 01 | Expensive*

### TRATTORIA CANZONE

Pizza in a charming old town trattoria; a huge selection and very good quality.

The remains of the Roman Forum can be made out in front of the 1200-year-old round church of Sv. Donat

*Stomorica 8 | tel. 023 21 20 81 | Budget–Moderate*

## SHOPPING

The markets are a special experience. From early in the morning until noon the catch of the day is traded in the ● *fish market hall* on the harbour side within the town wall. Next door the farmers from the surrounding area come to the *Colourful Market* to sell their fruit and vegetables.

## ENTERTAINMENT

The streets and cafés in the INSIDER TIP Varoš neighbourhood between Ulica Špire Brusine and Obala Petra Krešimira are Zadar's fashionable meeting places. The jeunesse dorée relax in more elegant style in INSIDER TIP *Arsenal*, a Venetian naval base that has been transformed into a lounge bar. The café bar and restaurant, which serve delicious snacks, are the meeting place of Zadar's in-crowd until 3am. From time to time the Arsenal also hosts live music events as well as frequent private events *(Trg tri bunara 1 | tel. 023 25 38 33 | www.arsenalzadar.com)*. For some time now the well-styled, modern *Shine* has been giving this cult address a run for its money; during the day it is a café and lounge, in the evenings it is transformed into a cocktail bar with DJs *(M. Pavlinovića 16 | tel. 09 13 99 96 01)*.

## WHERE TO STAY

**FALKENSTEINER HOTELS & RESIDENCES**
This holiday resort chain runs the family-friendly *Club Funimation (258 rooms)*, which has a particularly large number of

# BOOKS & FILMS

▶ **Dubrovnik: A History** – Robin Harris's readable, well-researched insights into a turbulent history that will surprise readers who have little previous knowledge of the city.

▶ **Croatia: A Nation Forged in War** – President Franjo Tudjman spoke of the Croats' 'thousand-year-old dream of independence'. Marcus Tanner, the former Balkan correspondent of the The Independent, looks at the story of the Croats from the early Middle Ages and describes how this dream finally came true in the 1990s.

▶ **Black Lamb and Grey Falcon** – Rebecca West, a redoubtable Englishwoman, and her banker husband travelled round Yugoslavia in the 1930s. She recorded her impressions in a fascinating account, which includes some enchanting passages on, for example, Diocletian's palace in Split.

▶ **Winnetou 1–3** – Lex Barker as Old Shatterhand with French actor Pierre Brice as his helper, an Apache chief, in classic precursors to the spaghetti western genre that were filmed on this coast, for example in Paklenica Gorge, at the Krka cascades near Skradin and in Dubrovnik's hinterland.

▶ **Croatia Cruising Companion (Wiley Nautical)** – A bible for Adriatic sailors: details of the mainland coastline and islands off Croatia, with thorough explanations of the pros and cons of various anchorages.

Melons, peaches, peppers: the vitamins are piled up high on Zadar market

activities on offer for active holidaymakers. Guests will find a stylish ambience in a quiet atmosphere in the *Adriana Select (48 junior suites). Majstora Radovana 7 | tel. 023 20 66 36 | www.falkensteiner. com | Expensive*

### PANSION MARIA
The family-run guesthouse situated somewhat outside of Zadar with accommodation in small but attractively furnished rooms with balconies. *12 rooms | Put Petrića 24 | tel. 023 33 42 45 | www. pansionmaria.hr | Budget*

### VILLA HREŠĆ ☆
This small privately-owned hotel on Maestral Bay has two modern rooms, six apartments and marvellous views of the old town. *Obala kneza Trpimira 28 | tel. 023 33 75 70 | www.villa-hresc.hr | Moderate).*

## SPORTS & LEISURE

### CANOE SAFARI ON THE ZRMANJA
Around 50 km (31 mi) east of Zadar a canoe trip through the deep Zrmanja Gorge and a refreshing shower under the gushing Jankobića waterfall bring back memories of Winnetou and Old Shatterhand. This wild setting was the location for some scenes of the Western. Can be booked through *Val Tours (tel. 023 38 64 79 | www. val-tours.hr) among others.*

## BOAT CONNECTIONS

The *Zadar–Ancona (Italy)* ferry runs up to seven times a week during the peak season, *Zadar–Preko/Ugljan* every 1–2 hours during the day, *Zadar–Brbinj/Dugi otok* and *Zaglav/Dugi otok* several times a day. Foot-passenger ferries depart daily from Zadar for the archipelago's car-free islands.

## INFORMATION

### TOURIST INFO
*Narodni trg 1 | tel. 023 316166 | www. tzzadar.hr*

## WHERE TO GO

### IŽ (130 C4–5) (*Ø E3*)
A good 5 km (3.1 mi) surfaced road connects the car ferry terminal of Bršanj with

the most important villages on the green island (18 sq km, 7 sq mi), *Veli Iž* and *Mali Iž*. Three-quarters of the 650 islanders live in the main village of Veli Iž. It has a small harbour, a pebble beach as well as a proper theatre that was opened in 1927. The best place to eat is INSIDER TIP *Mandrač (tel. 023 27 71 15 | Budget)*, an insider tip among sailors on account of its hearty meat dishes. The island's only hotel, 🙂 *Korinjak*, is a plain, utilitarian building,

sites such as *www.molat.comuv.com*. There are no hotels here, but you will be rewarded with deserted beaches and tranquil villages, where everyday life is governed by the fields and the sea.

*Molat* (population: 222), with its almost 30 sq km, 11.6 sq mi) and three villages is already one of the larger islands in this group; it is ideal for all those seeking restorative days and welcoming hospitality.

Shallow water and an (almost) deserted beach in Nin's lagoon

which pursues a holistic approach, offering vegetarian cuisine and a large choice of yoga and meditation sessions *(80 rooms | Veli Iž | tel. 023 27 70 64 | www.korinjak. hr | Moderate)*. *Iška keramika,* household items made of clay and stonemeal, are fired in traditional manner over an open fire in the village's last pottery. *Information: Tourist Info Zadar | Crossing: 1 hr 50 mins from Zadar*

### MOLAT ARCHIPELAGO
(130 B–C4) (*ഡ D3*)

Trips from the mainland to the car-free islands of *Ist, Molat, Zverinac, Sestrunj* and *Rivanj* are often only possible with an overnight stay in private accommodation, which can be booked through

*Information: Tourist Info Zadar | Crossing: depending on the island 35 mins–2.5 hrs from Zadar*

### NIN/ZATON (130 C4) (*ഡ E3*)

As a welcome greeting a loaf of bread and a wine bottle are chiselled into the stone of the right-hand side of the town gate (17th century). Behind it the more than 2800-year-old Nin (population: 1700) leads a dreamy existence in a sandy lagoon on its 500-square-metre island, which is connected to the mainland via two bridges. Called Aenona in Antiquity, Nin was the main settlement of the Illyrian Liburnians. On the ruins of the town, which once had a population of more than 45,000, the immigrant Croats built a new town in the 7th century and made it both the spiritual and intellectual centre of their early medieval kingdom.

The 9th-century hexagonal stone Višeslav font was found in Nin. The first Slavic princes had themselves baptized in it by Frankish missionaries. A replica can be found in the small Archaeological Museum of Nin *(May/June, Sept Mon–Sat 9am–noon, 5pm–8pm, July–Aug 9am–10pm, winter 8am–2pm | 12 kunas)*, while the original can be viewed in Split. The pre-Romanesque church of Sv. Kriz, also called the smallest cathedral in the world, dates back to the same era and is a nice example of ancient Croatian church architecture. *Branimir (Višeslavov trg 2 | tel. 023 26 48 66 | Moderate)* restaurant serves excellent, inexpensive fare in addition to a view of this architectural gem.

The wild sandy beaches around Nin have remained largely undiscovered by tourists so far. They only tend to be frequented at the weekends by local bathers and surfers. Conditions at these sandy beaches are ideal. The *windsurfing centre Surf-mania* hires out equipment and offers courses for windsurfers and kitesurfers *(15 April–15 Nov | Ninske Vodice | tel. 098 9 12 98 18 | www.surfmania.hr)*. The healing mud that can be found in a few locations is considered to be an effective treatment for rheumatism.

2 km (1.2 mi) from Nin is the two-storey *Zaton* apartment complex, built around a wide pebbly bay that gets very busy during the summer months. The complex also has a large, very well equipped campsite, several restaurants, bars, shops, tennis courts, a riding stable and one of Croatia's largest nightclubs, *Saturnus (www.disco-saturn.com)*, as well as a small pleasure-boat harbour and a very nice beach *(553 apartments | tel. 023 28 02 80 | www.zaton.hr | Moderate–Expensive)*. *Information: Tourist Info | Nin | tel. 023 26 42 80 | www.nin.hr. | 16 km (9.9 mi) to the northwest*

## SILBA (130 A–B3) (*D2*)

The island of Silba is only around 15 sq km (5.8 sq mi). During the seafaring golden age, rich captains had several magnificent villas built in the only island settlement. The hexagonal 'Tower of Love' (Toretta), built by a captain in the 17th century for his beloved, dates from a time when Silba had more than 3500 inhabitants. Today there are only 300. Thanks to the sheltered harbour Silba has made a name for itself among the sailing community. Anyone coming to this island will find small, remote bathing bays, accessible via trails. The 350 beds in rooms and apartments are available from private individuals. *Information: Silba | tel. 023 37 01 75 | www.silba.net | Crossing: 1hr, 35 mins from Zadar*

The 'Tower of Love' of Silba

# SPLIT REGION

Central Dalmatia, the place the Roman emperor Diocletian chose for his retirement 1700 years ago, still remains one of Dalmatia's most popular holiday regions, wowing visitors with its maquis-covered islands of Hvar, Brač and Vis, its wide pebble bays along the Makarska Riviera and the mountainous hinterland of the Biokovo .

Its lively heart is the port of Split, home of Diocletian's palace; stone-built Trogir has lots of historical treasures.

# BRAČ

(132–133 C–D4) (*m* H–J 5–6) The famous 'Brač marble', snow-white limestone, has been an unfading witness to events on the island since Antiquity.

Fashioned into walls, it encloses centres of wealth and power: Diocletian's palace in Split, Šibenik Cathedral and Trogir Cathedral, the Reichstag in Berlin, the parliament in Vienna, magnificent palaces in Venice and even the White House in Washington D.C. Brač is Croatia's third-largest island, with a total area of 395 sq km (152 sq mi) (max. 40 km (24.9 mi) long, 13 km (8.1 mi) wide), and it also has the country's highest mountains. The majority of the 14,000 inhabitants live in around two dozen towns, most of which are situated on the northern coast, only 7 km (4.3 mi) from the mainland. Towards the interior, the rounded landmass rises up in terraces to the plateau of *Vidova gora* (up

---

Photo: Split's old town

City flair and bathing fun:
lively ports, cosy konobas and
remote beaches

to 700 m), covered in European black pines, until reaching the peak of *Vidovica* (778 m), the highest on Brač. Around the town and in the valleys farmers have laboriously cultivated the meagre soil to grow wine, fruit and olives. The steep southwest coast is lined by Aleppo pine woods. The characteristic image of Brač is shaped, however, by the remote, barren landscape of maquis, woods and karst, in which the eternal sound of crickets sounds like a mystical song.

## PLACES ON BRAČ

### BOL (133 D4) *(𝄞 H6)*

Bol (population: 1300), the oldest town on Brač's south coast, lies at the foot of the steep *Bolska kruna* mountain range. Its main tourist attraction is ★ ● *Zlatni rat* (Golden Cape), a 500 m (547 yd) green promontory surrounded by golden sand, whose tip is always shifting by the power of the wind and the waves. Surfers appreciate the favourable winds in *Hvarski kanal (Hvar Channel)*, which runs between Brač and the island of Hvar. Their haunts are the beaches of Potočine and Borak to the west of Bol on the way to Zlatni Rat. Among the many windsurfing schools, Big Blue has made a good name for itself *(www.big-blue-sport.hr)*.

net/bol/villagiardino | *Moderate)*. Sports enthusiasts will enjoy the broad spectrum of activities, from windsurfing to speedboating and beach volleyball, on offer at Aloha campsite 2.5 km (1.6 mi) from Zlatni Rat beach *(Mara Marulića 3 |*

'Golden Cape': the popular beach of Zlatni rat on the southern coast of Brač

It is located directly next to Hotel Borak and also hires out mountain bikes and sea kayaks.

Several hotel complexes have been built around small bays along the shady waterfront promenade that connects Zlatni Rat with the town centre (30-minute walk). One of them is Hotel Borak, a comfortable 4-star wellness complex with 136 bright, modern rooms and 48 apartments *(Bračka cesta 13 | tel. 021 30 62 02 | www.bluesunhotels.com | Expensive)*. A spot for romantics: in a small side street above the harbour is the ornately furnished INSIDER TIP *Villa Giardino* in a Mediterranean garden *(14 rooms | Novi Put 2 | tel. 021 63 59 00 | www.dalmacija.*

tel. 021 63 53 67 | www.nautic-center-bol. com | *Budget)*.

The area around the small harbour of Bol is a vibrant part of town. *Galerija Dešković* exhibits works by older and contemporary Croatian painters and sculptors *(June–Sept daily 6pm–11pm | 10 kunas)*. A short walk from the harbour is the romantic garden restaurant called *Ranč (tel. 021 63 56 35 | Moderate)*: the Lukšić family will serve you fresh grilled crayfish in a cosy environment. The rustic konoba *Mlin*, an old oil mill, is one of Bol's top restaurants *(Ante Starčevića 11 | tel. 021 63 53 76 | Moderate)*. All year round the café bar *Aquarius* and *Varadero Lounge* are meeting places for young people and windsurfers in particular. During the summer months people come to the *Faces Club Kaltemberg* to dance until the early hours of the morning.

To the east of the harbour, on the small *Glavica* peninsula, is a *Dominican priory* (15th century). The collection in the monastery museum includes the altarpiece 'The Madonna Between the Saints', a work by Tintoretto (1518–94). *Daily 9am–noon, 5pm–7pm | 12 kunas*

Outside of the summer months Bol is an ideal base for hiking trips across Brač. One popular hiking destination *(distance approx. 3 hrs)* is the *Blaca Hermitage*. It was established in the 16th century and houses monks' cells, an observatory and valuable old books *(Tue–Sun 9am–5pm | 30 kunas)*. From ☀ *Vidova gora* plateau you get views across the entire island and of the imposing coastal mountains on the mainland, as well as the rugged coastline of the neighbouring island of Hvar.

In the hamlet of *Gornji Humac* 10 km (6.2 mi) away, the houses are still cov-

ered in whitewashed stone slabs. The ☺ INSIDERTIP *Konoba Tomić (tel. 021 64 72 42 | www.konobatomic.com | Moderate)* grills its meat on an open fire, while the bread comes from a wood-fired oven and the vegetables from its own garden. There are pretty bathing bays all around the hamlet of *Murvica* 4 km (2.5 mi) away. They can only be reached on foot. There is also a mysterious INSIDERTIP *dragon's den* with Glagolitic and pagan inscriptions and paintings. Viewings are organized by Mr Zoran *(tel. 091 514 97 87 | approx. 50 kunas)*. *Information: Tourist Info | Porat bolskih pomoraca | Bol | tel. 021 63 56 38 | www.bol.hr*

## MILNA (132 C4) (*ω H5–6*)

The palatial buildings around the harbour basin in this small town on Brač's west coast are reminiscent of the island's golden age. In the mid-19th century large trading vessels were built in Milna. Today the sheltered ACI marina is particularly popular with amateur skippers and their yachts. A few taverns and café

---

**MARCO POLO HIGHLIGHTS**

bars as well as small shops for daily essentials are sufficient for the few guests who come to Milna. Apartments with a friendly character are let by *Illyrian Resort (59 apartments | tel. 021 63 65 66 | www. illyrian-resort.hr | Moderate)*. Mackerel, seafood and also pizza in the evenings are served on the shady terrace of *Fontana,* a restaurant by the harbour *(Žalo | tel. 021 63 62 85 | Budget–Moderate)*.

On the way from Milna through the heart of the island to Bol, you will pass through *Donji Humac,* where the small INSIDER TIP *Jakšić galery* exhibits works by this incredibly creative family, whose men are now the third generation working as sculptors *(tel. 021 64 77 10 | www. drazen-jascic.hr)*. *Information Milna: Tourist Info | Milna | tel. 021 63 62 33*

### PUČIŠĆA (133 D4) (*Ⓜ H5*)

Sheltered from the stormy attacks of the icy bora, the harbour lies hidden at the centre of Pučišća at the end of a fjord-like bay. The limestone from the nearby quarries has dominated life here since time immemorial. On the left of the harbour basin *(Nova Riva)*, Croatia's only school of stonemasonry has been training apprentices in this ancient craft for more than a hundred years. These days they also include women. If stylish accommodation is what you want, then the Renaissance *Desković Palace (tel. 021 77 82 40 | www.palaca-deskovic.com | Expensive)* with 15 rooms and a restaurant is for you.

### ŠKRIP (133 D4) (*Ⓜ H5*)

The historic part of town, situated on a hill north of Nerežišća, has a church tower, a castle and large defensive towers, making it feel rather like an old fairytale castle. Sarcophaguses and the Bassin carved into the solid rock with the animal trough and the small, ancient 10th-century Chapel of the Holy Spirit all date back to Roman times, when hundreds of slaves worked in the quarries here.

*Radojković Tower*, which was built on a well-preserved Roman mausoleum (3rd century), now houses Brač's museum. The highlight is a Roman stone relief depicting Hercules *(June–Sept daily 8am–8pm | 12 kunas | if it is locked, knock next door where the Radojković family live)*.

### SUPETAR (132 C4) (*Ⓜ H5*) The car ferries from Split dock in the new harbour.

# BRIGHT WHITE

There is evidence that Brač's limestone, often falsely believed to be marble, has been quarried since the time of Emperor Diocletian, i.e. since the 3rd century. It is likely that the people who settled here before the Romans also used the white stone, because it possesses two great advantages: it is relatively soft, which means it is easy to 'harvest' as the people of Brač say, and it is equally easy to work. It also hardens over time, which makes the buildings it was used for more stable. The walls of Diocletian's Palace in Split are elegant testimony to this. This stone is still quarried in several locations on the island; it is sold by companies such as Jadrankamen, based in Pušćića. Among the many sculptors who work with Brač limestone, *Dražen Jakšić* stands out. He exhibits his works in a gallery in Donji Humac.

Main tourist centre on the island of Brač: the lively town of Supetar (pop. 3000)

Buses departing to all of the island's towns leave from the waterfront. Su petar is the island's economic, cultural and tourist centre. The rustic little homes with their small windows and high chimneys in the old town centre of the former fishing and farming village are now surrounded by modern villas and weekend houses. In the small church there are two sarcophaguses from the early Christian period, surrounded by graves with sculptures belonging to rich villagers.

Between the headland and Vela Luka Bay lies Supetar's tourist centre. Behind the shallow pebble bays of Uvala Banj and *Vlačica beach*, a park-like pine grove provides some welcome shade. The coastline (rock and pebbles) to the west of Bili rat headland around *Vela Luka bay* has been left in a more natural state. Here too pine trees provide some pleasant shade. Contemporary design and interiors characterize the hotel complex of

the *Velaris Tourist Resort* in Vela Luka bay. You can choose between rooms in the modern main building or in the early 20th century villa. A tasteful garden leads down to the rock and pebble beach; the diving school adjoining the hotel, Amber, organizes excursions *(86 rooms, 6 apartments | Put Vela Luke 10 | tel. 021 60 66 06 | www.velaris.hr | Moderate–Expensive)*. If you are looking for more individual accommodation, you will find it in the family-run *Villa Adriatica (24 rooms | Put Vele Luke 31 | tel. 021 34 38 06 | www.villaadriatica.com | Moderate)*. This hotel, decorated in warm colours, also has a good restaurant and the smart *Sunshine Café.*

Dalmatian delicacies, such as homemade fish paste, crabs and lobster are served in the cosy old wine cellar *Vinotoka (Jobova 6 | tel. 021 63 09 69 | Moderate)*. Kiwi vines and pomegranate trees are an attractive addition to the terrace of the restaurant *Jastog*. In addition to fish and meat, Miro also prepares vegetables for the vegetarian selection on the open charcoal grill *(Bana Josipa Jelačiča 6 | tel. 021 63 14 86 | Moderate)*. Information: Tourist Info | Porat 1 | Supetar | tel. 021 63 05 51 | www.supetar.hr

Several kilometres further east, in *Splitska (133 D4) (᠁ H5)* – in Roman times the export harbour for Brač stone, which was used in construction directly opposite, in modern-day Split – the islands have not yet been impacted so severely by tourism. The small town, which has been built on the steep slopes rising up from a deep bay, is a peaceful idyll where no hotel has (yet) established itself. Accommodation can be found through the tourist office in Supetar. It is worth visiting the studio of sculptor *Ive Kora,* who creates interesting sculptures from olive wood in the neighbouring *Postira (tel. 021 63 21 35 | www.ivekora.com)*.

## BOAT CONNECTIONS

The connection *Split–Supetar/Brač* runs up to eleven times a day during the peak season, while the connection *Makarska–Sumartin/Brač* runs up to six times a day during the summer.

# HVAR

*(132–133 C–E 4–5) (᠁ H–J6)* **Hvar consists of turquoise bays, olive groves, vineyards, green pine forests and the enchanting scents of rosemary and lavender.**

Attractive churches and palaces in the historic town are evidence of its former power. In the villages the rustic homes of the farmers and fishermen are simple and functional. Every one of these typically Mediterranean details can be found all over the Dalmatian islands. However, on the island of Hvar they come together perfectly to create an impressive ambience.

This 'slender beauty' is around 70 km (43.5 mi) long and between 4 (2.5 mi) to 11 km (6.8 mi) wide. Hvar gets an incredible 2724 hours of sunshine a year. It is no problem for the 11,000 permanent inhabitants to accommodate more than twice that number of holidaymakers. Guests come all year round, because even in the winter the climate is pleasantly mild.

Tourism focuses on the areas of interest around the four main towns on the island, all of which are in the north of Hvar. They are the town of *Hvar* on the side of the island that looks out to the sea, *Stari Grad, Vrboska* and *Jelsa*, which face the mainland. In recent years the town of Hvar has developed into one of the preferred haunts of the international jetset. The yachts of the rich and famous in the town's harbour are impressive! This has had an impact on the prices and the atmosphere. This place is right for those who like to party the nights away in fancy clubs and while away the daytime hours in beach lounges. If it is peace and quiet you are after, then you are better off in the more tranquil *Stari Grad*.

There is a 1000-metre, single-lane tunnel near *Pitve* that leads to *Zavala, Ivandolac* and *Sv. Nedjelja*, all of which are villages comprising the municipality of Jelsa. A set of lights regulates traffic through the tunnel. These small fishing villages that are away from the busy tourist hotspots are very popular with surfers and divers. The island is almost uninhabited between Jelsa and its eastern end, *Sućuraj, 43 km (26.7 mi)* away. During the day the old ☙ winding road has great views of the Adriatic and the island of Brač opposite. This road is not used by many cars anymore. That has made it all the more popular with mountain bikers and scooter riders.

### HVAR (TOWN) ★ (132 C4) (*H6*)

You will get the best view of the whole panorama of this Mediterranean gem and 18th centuries. The Venetian fleet used to overwinter In the sheltered harbour of Hvar. Now cruise ships and yachts come with passengers from all around the world in order to experience the town's swanky flair for a few hours. To the right of the small, old harbour basin is the large main square, *Trg Sv. Stjepana*,

A 'butterfly dreaming on waves' – the sunny island of Hvar

(population: 4000) from the water. By looking at the town from a distance, you get the best impression of the palm-lined waterfront promenade and the 700-year-old defensive walls that run up the slope all the way to the 16th century Tvrđava *Španjol (Spanish Fort, summer daily 8am–midnight | 20 kunas)*. Above it is Napoleon Fort, built by the French in 1811. The most important churches, monasteries and palaces all date back to Hvar's golden age, when the naval power Venice took over the town and developed it into an important base in the eastern Adriatic between the 15th whose paving stones have become shiny with age. At the front of the square is the Cathedral of St Stephen, *Katedrala Sv. Stjepan* (built between the 13th and 18th centuries) with its openwork tracery tower.

Hvar has been a diocese for 850 years. The cathedral treasure, consisting of documents, paintings, liturgical vestments and utensils, can be viewed in the bishop's palace next door *(summer daily 10am–noon, 5pm–7pm | 15 kunas)*. The main square is also home to the large city well, built in 1520. You should definitely try sea-devil carpaccio at the Hanibal, a restaurant on the square *(tel. 021 74 27 60 | Moderate)*.

A large arch, 10 metres wide, covers the gate of the Arsenal, which looks out over the harbour. The Venetian military galleys used to be repaired here. The small theatre, one of the first public stages of the modern era in Europe, was built above the Arsenal in 1612 *(summer daily 9am–1pm, 3pm–11pm | 15 kunas)*. The neighbouring rooms feature an exhibition of contemporary Croatian art. The Hotel Palace, built in 1903, is reminiscent of the city loggia with its clock tower and magnificent façade; it has tastefully modernized rooms and a wonderful café terrace *(73 rooms | tel. 021 74 19 66 | www.suncanihvar.hr | Moderate)*.

Towards the sea, to the right, trails lead through the park to the Amfora hotel complex *(320 rooms | tel. 021 75 03 00 | Expensive)*. Around 200 m away a largely young clientele spend the nights partying in the Veneranda open-air nightclub *(daily midnight–5am | from 30 kunas)*.

On the harbour basin's east side sailors like to be admired on their elegant yachts. Only a few steps above the promenade is *Carpe Diem*, where you can sip colourful cocktails to quiet bar music. Somewhat further along the promenade, the friars of the ● *Franciscan priory* (15th century) exhibit their treasures: an extensive botanical collection, paintings by old masters and handwritten books *(summer Mon–Sat 9am–3pm | 20 kunas)*. During the summer months the cloister is transformed into an atmospheric venue for classical music concerts.

The Groda neighbourhood on the northern side of the main square is home to Benedictine nuns **INSIDER TIP** who produce fine bobbin lace doilies from threads spun from the fibres of agave leaves. The best pieces are on display in a small museum, where the nuns also sell their filigree treasures *(June–Sept Mon–Fri 10am–noon, 5pm–7pm | 10*

Hvar: as is often the case on the Adriatic, the harbour promenade is also the place to enjoy a stroll

*kunas)*. There are also some cosy restaurants in this neighbourhood, such as the Macondo *(tel. 021 74 28 50 | Moderate)*, where you can enjoy a warming fire during cooler weather. The Croatian tapas – grilled sardines, spicy sausage and aromatic sheep's cheese – served in Menego, an intimate tavern, are definitely worth trying *(Groda, tel. 021 74 20 36 | Moderate)*.

When INSIDER TIP the lavender is in bloom from June to September bees come out en masse to the lavender fields around the village of Brusje 6 km (3.7 mi) north of Hvar. Almost every house then starts selling lavender products and a aromatic lavender honey.

The densely forested offshore islands of Pakleni otoci are popular for their attractive swimming beaches on the southern side. Taxi boats *(approx. 50 kunas)* depart from the harbour to Sv. Klement or Jerolim (naturist beach). The Carpe Diem Club runs its own shuttle service to its INSIDER TIP *Carpe Diem Beach* in Stipanska Bay on the island of *Marinkovac*, where a restaurant, a lounge bar, a pool, elegant wooden loungers and various DJs spoil the sunworshippers *(May–Sept 8am–8pm, until midnight for events | www.carpe-diem-hvar.com)*.

Inexpensive, quiet accommodation can be found 5 km (3.1 mi) north of Hvar on Lozna Bay: Laguna Lozna is a guesthouse and diving base that has several pleasant rooms and apartments *(6 rooms, 4 apartments | tel. 022 48 52 31 | www.hvar-lozna.com | Budget). Information: Tourist Info | Trg Sv. Stjepana | Hvar | tel. 021 74 29 77 | www.hvar.hr*

## MILNA (132 C5) *(ꕤ H6)*
This village is situated on the island's southern coast, 4 km (2.5 mi) east of Hvar (bus connection). The ⚹ trail, a marked path through the Mediterranean maquis vegetation along the sea, takes around 2 hours. A tranquil place with a small beach, a few private apartments, a grocery store and a number of restaurants. They alone warrant the trip, because the food here is still typically Dalmatian and the prices are good too at, for example, Ivo and Sibe Tudor's in *Kod Barba Božjeg,* which has a nice terrace overlooking the sea *(rooms also available | tel. 021 74 50 45 | Budget)*. The beautiful beaches and the wide pebbly bays right in Milna and the bays of Malo and *Veliko Borče* to the north of the village are also worth visiting.

## STARI GRAD (133 D4) *(ꕤ H6)*
The centre of this town, which is surrounded by vineyards, is situated at the end of a 6 km (3.7 mi) fjord-like bay. Stari Grad (population: 1700) is the oldest settlement on Hvar, founded by the Greeks in the 4th century BC under the name of Paros. Their victory over the Illyrians, who were already inhabiting the area, is attested by a plaque in the museum of the Dominican priory *(June–Sept daily 10am–noon, 6pm–7.30pm, May, Oct 10am–12pm, 5pm–7pm | 12 kunas)*. The exhibition also has an interesting painting created by the Venetian master Tintoretto for the Croatian poet Petar Hektorović in the 16th century. The INSIDER TIP sacred painting immortalizes the poet himself as well as his daughter Lucrezia.

Hektorović's former country estate is situated on the harbour promenade. In the palace's courtyard an arcaded walkway surrounds the fishpond that is fed with seawater and inhabited by mullets. Allegedly it will rain if they all swim in a circle. The garden's jewel is a magnolia that is more than 100 years old *(daily June/Sept 10am–1pm, July/Aug also 5pm–8pm | 12 kunas)*.

Archaeology fans will be interested to know that around the small 6th century church of Sv. Ivan remains of the old town wall from the Greco-Illyrian period were uncovered and preserved. These works are documented in Biankini Palace *(June–Sept daily 10am–noon, 7pm–9pm | 20 kunas)*.

In 2008 ● Stari Grad Plain, a fertile karst valley between Stari Grad and Jelsa, was declared a Unesco World Heritage Site, because the vineyards and olive groves are still divided into the same plots that were created by the *Greek colonists* in the 4th century BC: it consists of 75 parcels approximately 181 x 905 m, which are in turn divided into five square fields measuring 181 x 181 m. The stone walls surrounding these fields and the shelters for the farmers are also based on ancient models.

Food and accommodation can be found in Stari Grad proper. Culinary treats, such as tuna braised in capers and white whine, are served in the cosy Antika *(tel. 021 76 54 79 | Moderate)*. The accommodation options include private rooms (information from the Tourist Info) and the idyllic little campsite, run by the Lusić family in the hamlet of Mudri Dolac, 8 km (5 mi) towards Jelsa. The ten pitches are right by the water; there is also an apartment available in the house *(tel. 09 15 01 89 24 | www.mudridolac.com | Budget)*. *Information: Tourist Info | Nova Riva 2 | Stari Grad | tel. 021 76 57 63 | www.stari-grad-faros.hr*

## VRBOSKA/JELSA (133 D4) (𝄞 H6)

These two fishing villages, picturesquely situated in sheltered, forested bays, are connected to each other via an approx. 1.5 km (0.9 mi) trail along the coast (Lungomare). The drive from Jelsa to Vrboska is around 5 km (3.1 mi). Regular visitors prefer the private accommodation. There are some nice old townhouses as well as the Baroque church of Sv. Ivan around Jelsa's (population: 1700) town square. The friendly guesthouse Murvica *(5 apts. | tel. 021 76 14 05 | www.murvica.net | Budget)* can be recommended; its restaurant serves very good Dalmatian delicacies *(Moderate)*. Families and children will appreciate the fine sandy beach in *Mina Bay*.

On a small hill above the old town in the village of Vrboska (population: 500) is the nearly windowless fortress church of Sv. Marija (16th century) with its two defensive towers. The altar painting is now in the parish church of Sv. Lovrinac (15th century). Some believe it could be a work by Titian or Paolo Veronese. The small *fishing museum* by contrast illustrates the history of fishing on Hvar with an array of items *(daily 10am–1pm, 6pm–9pm, except Wed evenings | 12 kunas)*.

## LOW BUDGET

▶ Hvar (town) is one of the most expensive spots on the Croatian Adriatic coast; *The Green Lizard* provides a welcome change. The pleasantly furnished double rooms and shared rooms are clean and inexpensive. *Lucica bb | tel. 021 74 25 60 | www.greenlizard.hr*

▶ In a city with as many museums and attractions as Split, it is easy to spend lots of money on admission fees. Get a *Split Card (37 kunas, free if you're staying three days or longer)* to benefit from free or reduced entry fees as well as further discounts in hotels and restaurants *(www.split-info.hr)*.

The pebble beach in *Maslinica Bay* north of the village has turquoise blue water and is considered one of the most beautiful on the island.

In the hamlet of *Sv. Nedjelja* on the west coast, Zlatan Plenkovic produces the island's best wines; his **INSIDER TIP** 'Zlatan otok' can be sampled in the konoba *Bilo Idro (tel. 021 74 57 09 | Moderate)*. Try it with fresh fish or a starter plate of *pršut* and cheese. *Information: Tourist Info Vrboska | tel. 021 77 41 37 | www.vrboska. info; Tourist Info Jelsa | tel. 021 76 10 17 | www.tzjelsa.hr*

**vineyards and olive groves huddle together on a narrow, fertile strip between the Adriatic and the *Biokovo Mountains*.** Its highest peak, the rugged Sveti Jure, rises a majestic 1762 m (1927 yd) into the sky. The steep karst walls rise up on the island's seaward side like a powerful bastion, bare and ochre. This contrast in a very small area is the most striking characteristic of the 60 km (37.3 mi) Makarska Riviera, which is probably the most beautiful holiday region of the central Dalmatian mainland coast.

Beyond Brela, the northernmost town

We're almost there: evening mood on the ferry to Hvar

## BOAT CONNECTIONS

There are several ferries a day between *Split–Stari Grad/Hvar* and between *Drvenik–Sućuraj/Hvar*, while the coastal ferry *Rijeka–Dubrovnik* departs daily from *Stari Grad/Hvar*, and there is a bi-weekly service during the peak season *Ancona (Italy)–Stari Grad/Hvar*.

# MAKARSKA RIVIERA

(133 D–F 4–5) (∅ H–K 5–6) **Beyond white pebbly bays lined by green pine forests,**

on the Makarska Riviera, there are *Baška Voda, Promajna, Makarska, Tučepi, Podgora, Igrane, Živogošće, Drvenik, Zaostrog* and *Gradac*. All of these seaside towns also have a higher counterpart directly below the rock walls. For centuries these refuges were used by the coastal inhabitants to hide from pirates and hostile conquerors trying to attack and invade them. A few of these small houses, nestled close together under the cliffs, are still inhabited today.

With its many accommodation options, marinas, playing fields and restaurants, the Makarska Riviera is a lively holiday region and one that often gets noisy, particularly during the peak season.

### BAŠKA VODA (133 E4) (*∅ J5*)

This much-visited holiday town is one of the oldest on the Makarska Riviera. Grapes, olives, cherries and figs grow inland. Baška Voda reaches all the way to the neighbouring Brela. Located right on the beach and surrounded by pine trees, the comfortable *Hotel Horizont* pampers guests with its spa *(202 rooms | tel. 021 60 49 99 | www.hoteli-baskavoda.hr | Expensive)*. For a hearty meal, drive up to the konoba *Biston (tel. 091 2 52 22 79 | Budget)* in the little village of *Bast*.

### BRELA ★ (133 D4) (*∅ J5*)

Idyllic picture-postcard beaches: Brela's trademarks are its white pebble bays, lined by lavish pine forests which climb up the base of the slopes. The sand and pebble beach of *Punta Rata* is famous: framed by rocks and pine trees, it is a picture-book idyll. Rooms and apartments are available in most of the newly built, elegant villas around the old, neat centre. Whether it is wind surfing, water skiing or canoeing, you will find several sports-equipment providers on Brela's beaches. The Adriatic Highway runs above the town. The first building on the square is *Hotel Soline (206 rooms | tel. 021 60 30 20 | www.bluesunhotels.com | Moderate–Expensive)*, right on the beach. The hotel possesses a pleasant spa with an indoor pool, in which the guests can swim through a recreated 'Blue Grotto' into the outdoor pool. The konoba Feral at the harbour is Brela's best address for freshly caught fish *(Obala Kneza Domagoka | tel. 021 6189 09 | Moderate–Expensive)*. In the evenings the beach bar Southern Comfort, located on the beach towards Baška Voda, is a popular meeting place and an atmospheric one too, being lit by torches. *Information: Tourist Info | Trg Alojzija Stepinca | tel. 021 618455 | www.brela.hr*

### GORNJI TUČEPI & BIOKOVO MOUNTAINS (133 E4) (*∅ J5–6*)

Gornji Tučepi (Upper Tučepi) is the starting point for hikes up the highest peak of the Biokovo Mountains, the 1762 m (1927 yd) *Sveti Jure*. The climb will take at least three hours and should only be considered in good weather. It begins to the right of the village church. The right clothes and sufficient food and drink are important. There is a also a winding and quite dangerous road (40 km, 24.9 mi) that leads almost to the peak through the nature park *(toll: 35 kunas)*.

### MAKARSKA (133 E4) (*∅ J6*)

The historic town of Makarska (population: 17,000), after which the Riviera is named, is the regional tourist centre. A shady promenade connects more than half a dozen hotel resorts along the wide bay Donja luka all the way to the forested peninsula of Sv. Petar.

In addition to many other water sports on offer here, parasailing is a great way to experience the town in its setting in front of the Biokovo Mountains from an unusual perspective *(bookings: tel. 021 616125)*. If such heights are not for you, why not try the popular climbs along the cliffs on Osejava Peninsula, which are right on the water. You will find routes of every level of difficulty here. The most popular times for actively minded holidaymakers to walk or bike around the Makarska Riviera are spring and autumn. The terrace of the Susvid restaurant is attractively decorated with flowers; from here you can watch people go about their daily lives on the town's main square, while enjoying the dishes cooked up by Zdenko Vujčić, who prepares the

Rocks, pine trees and small bays shape the coastal landscape of the Makarska Riviera

meat dishes of the Biokovo (primarily lamb) and the fish dishes of the coast (brodetto) using traditional recipes *(Kačićev Trg 9 | tel. 021 612 7 32 | Moderate)*. Ivo is away from the hustle and bustle and somewhat less expensive, but the menu also features the typical dishes of the Biokovo *(Ante Starčevića 41 | tel. 021 611 2 57 | Budget–Moderate)*.

On the far side of the peninsula is the picturesque harbour with the quay for the car ferry to Sumartin on the island of Brač. The best views of the harbour are available from the small, elegant town hotel Biokovo, which is situated right on the harbour promenade. The hotel has a popular café with a large terrace in front of the building, from which you can observe life in this town *(54 rooms | Obala Kralja Tomislava | tel. 021 615 2 44 |*

*www.hotelbiokovo.hr | Moderate)*. Information: Tourist Info | Obala Kralja Tomislava | Makarska | tel. 021 612 0 02 | www.makarska-info.hr

Turning off from the highway, there is a small road leading up to the hamlet of *Mlinice*. The speciality in INSIDER TIP ▶ *Trattoria Mlinice* is Danilo's 'peka for friends', which he prepares with squid, fish or meat *(min. 4 people, must be ordered in advance | tel. 0915 81 48 36 | Moderate)*.

## OMIŠ (133 D3) *(ⴕ H5)*

The town of Omiš (population: 5000) is situated between the Makarska Riviera and Split, by the vast gorge that breaks through the Mosor Mountains and channels the water of the Cetina River to the sea. Before the town, part of the Kingdom of Bosnia, fell into Venetian hands in the

15th century the Narentines had their last headquarters here. Feared as pirates in the whole of the Adriatic for more than 500 years, they disappeared from history after the last punitive expedition in the 13th century. The ● INSIDER TIP *klapa choir* from Omiš is famous: the men are so good at Dalmatian a capella singing that they regularly win the competition at the klapa festival in July.

⚶ The views from the ruin of *Straigrad Fort*, 311 m (340 yd) above the town, are wonderful. The guests of the hotel Villa Dvor on the slopes of the old town *(23 rooms | tel. 021 86 34 44 | www.hotel-villadvor.hr | Moderate)* are blessed with an equally stunning panorama. It is worth driving a little way into the rugged, romantic *Cetina Gorge*. Small boats take half an hour from Omiš to the *Radmanove mlinice water mill*, a popular restaurant destination and starting point for good hikes through the green Mosor Mountains. *Information: Tourist Info | Trg Kneza Mislava | Omiš | tel. 021 86 13 50 | www.tz-omis.hr*

### TUČEPI (133 E4) (𝄐 J6)

Tučepi, with its 3 km (1.9 mi) pebble beach, is nowhere near as urban as Makarska, but it is still equally lively. Above the marina is the stylishly furnished *Hotel Laurentum (40 rooms, 3 apartments | Kraj 43 | tel. 021 60 59 00 | www.hotellaurentum.com | Moderate)*. From the town centre it is an approximately 45-minute walk up to the mountain village of *Gornji Tučepi*. Built in a wonderfully panoramic setting, this village is home to a gourmet oasis, namely ⚶ *Restaurant Jeny (Gornji Tucepi 22 | tel. 021 62 37 04 | www. restaurant-jeny.hr | Expensive)*, which serves light and creative Mediterranean cuisine. *Information: Tourist Info | Kraj 103 | Tučepi | tel. 021 62 31 00 | tucepi.com*

### RAFTING IN CETINA GORGE

Between Šestanovac and Zadvarje, in the hinterland of Omiš, you can go on an adventurous trip down the rapids of the Cetina River. The destination is most commonly the popular *Radmanove Milice. Information: Rafting association in Omiš | tel. 021 86 31 61 | www.raft.hr*

# SPLIT

### 🀫 MAP INSIDE THE BACK COVER

**(132 C3) (𝄐 H5) The magnificent Diocletian's Palace on the right-hand side of a row of buildings in the old quarter; in front of it the harbour promenade, lined by flowers, palm trees and colourful flags; to the left the green peninsula with *Marjan* hill; and in the water large**

**and small boats, gradually approaching this Mediterranean city.**

Split (population: 200,000) is Dalmatia's largest city, a city based on business and trade, administration and education, art and culture, it is a lively, modern place whose football club *Hajduk Split* is beloved by half of Croatia.

Split's cornerstone was laid by the Roman emperor Diocletian, a Romanized Illyrian (reigned: AD 284–305), who had a magnificent retirement palace built here, close to his home town of Salona (modern-day Solin). When Salona was later destroyed by immigrant Slavs and Avars, the population fled to the old palace and adapted it to their needs by converting, among other things, the mausoleum of the last Roman persecutor of Christians, Diocletian, into the cathedral of *Sv. Duje*. The Roman ruins excavated in *Solin* only allow experts to get an impression of the city's former significance.

> **CITY** **WHERE TO START?**
> The best starting point for a sightseeing tour is the waterfront promenade **Obala hrvatskoga narodnog preporoda**, or **Riva** for short, in front of Diocletian's Palace. There is also a car park here, but it is often full (there is an alternative on Vukovarska ulica). To the west of the palace is the old town around the lively **Narodni trg**.

## SIGHTSEEING

### ARCHAEOLOGICAL MUSEUM (ARHEOLOŠKI MUZEJ)

The best finds from the ancient ruins of Salona are on display here. *Mon–Sat 9am–2pm, 4pm–8pm (shorter in winter) | 20 kunas | Zrinjsko-Frankopanska ul. 25*

Cafés in front of Diocletian's Palace: Split owes its greatest attraction to the emperor who retired

Detail of Diocletian's Palace: Corinthian capitals crown the columns of the arcade

## DIOCLETIAN'S PALACE ★ ●

This Roman palace (180 x by 215 m) is the only surviving example anywhere and the most significant Roman building in the whole of Dalmatia. If you enter the palace via the Sea Gate, you will be able to make out the elaborate reconstructed basement vaults, which give an idea of the outline of the imperial quarters that once stood above them. Straight ahead, past the many jewellery and art stalls, is the peristyle, whose Corinthian columns frame the courtyard that is now occupied by a café. To the right of it is Sv. Duje cathedral, the converted mausoleum of Emperor Diocletian. To the left is the baptistery, the former Temple of Jupiter. Walking straight ahead from the peristyle, you will come through the Porta Aurea (Golden Gate) to the north side of the palace walls. There is an almost 8 m (8.7 yd) bronze statue by Ivan Meštrović here, of Bishop Gregory of Nin, who is an important figure for Croatia's early Christian history. INSIDER TIP It is said to bring good luck to touch his big toe. The *Porta Argentea* (Silver Gate) leads to the souvenir stalls along the palace wall and to the market on the eastern side. The old town is accessible via the *Porta Ferrea* (Iron Gate), which leads on to the *Narodni trg* (People's Square) with the old town hall *(reconstructed arches | daily 9am–6pm, winter 9am–2pm | 25 kunas)*.

## TEMPLE OF JUPITER/BAPTISTERY

The small 5th-century temple, which was converted into a Christian baptistery in the 9th century, is guarded by a stone sphinx. Its cruciform baptismal font is ornamented with the relief of a king sitting on his throne (11th century); a statue of John the Baptist, created by Meštrović, rises up above it. The barrel-shaped, stone coffered ceiling is quite unusual. *Mon–Sat 7am–noon, 5pm–7pm | 10 kunas*

## SV. DUJE CATHEDRAL ★ ●

This cathedral is an architectural masterpiece that master builders from the Byzantine era were involved in. At the heart of it is the octagonal mausoleum of the Roman emperor Diocletian, whose ornamented Corinthian columns now frame one of Dalmatia's most beautiful altars: Juraj Dalmatinac (Giorgio da Sebenico), the gifted Renaissance artist from Zadar, created the touching relief of the Flagellation of Christ in 1422. The richly decorated Roman portal is also of note. *Daily 8.30am–7.30pm | 15 kunas*

## MUSEUM OF CROATIAN ARCHAEO-LOGICAL MONUMENTS (MUZEJ HR-VATSKIH ARHEOLOŠKI SPOMENIKA)

This museum, housed in a modern building, contributes to an understanding of the Croats' historical awareness. Among the exhibits are the baptismal font from Nin (9th century) originally owned by Višeslav, the first Christian Croat ruler, and the sarcophagus of Queen Jelena, the wife of King Kresimir (10th century). Stone tablets depict typical symbols of old Croatian Christianity: birds with ears of corn, grapevines and olive tree leaves. *Mon–Fri 9am–4pm, Sat 9am–2pm | 10 kunas | Gunjačina*

## FOOD & DRINK

### BOBAN

Elegant and very dignified is the best description of one of Split's best fish restaurants. *Hektorovićeva 49 | tel. 021 54 33 00 | Expensive*

### BUFFET FIFE

This harbour bar is simple and jolly; the food served here is tasty home-cooked fare that comes in huge portions. Most of the tables here tend to be occupied. Among the people of Split the deep-fried little fish are an insider tip. *Closed Sun | Trumbićeva obala 11 | tel. 021 49 02 84 | Budget*

### ŠPERUN

Fish, like meat, is served well-prepared and tastily flavoured here. *Šperun 3 | tel. 021 34 69 99 | Moderate*

## SHOPPING

### GALERIJA FRESKA

The works by the Dalmatian painter Ante Mandarić are at the centre of the exhibition in this old town gallery. *Plinarska 49 | tel. 021 39 49 18 | www.galerija-freska.com*

### UJE ☺

This shop for natural products stocks a large selection of Croatian olive oils. *Kneza Viželslava 5 | tel. 021 49 09 90 | www.uje.hr*

## BEACHES

Split's city beach, *Bačvice* (pebbles / concrete), lies to the southeast of the old town and tends to be quite full; there is a rock and pebble beach at the foot of Marjan hill.

## ENTERTAINMENT

The evening begins in *Getto (Dosud 10)*, where you can sink into deep easy chairs between flowers and fountains. The young and beautiful can be found in *Tribu (Osmih Medite-ranskih Igara 3)* later at night, where international top DJs bring the mood to boiling point. The club's pool is the perfect place to cool down. Split's older party-goers tend to prefer the relaxed atmosphere in *Planet Jazz (Grgura Ninskog)*. Split's theatre programme includes opera, ballet and

Galerija Meštrović in Split:
the sculptor's former summer villa

lavish garden. The leisure options include an attractive ● Diocletian spa and wellness centre featuring an aroma grotto, a tennis academy, a water sports centre, a casino, eight restaurants and bars, a nightclub as well as a children's club. *Grljevacka 2 | Podstrana | tel. 021 50 05 00 | www.lemeridienlavsplit.com | Expensive*

### VILLA ANA
Familiar guesthouse in an old stone building, not far from the ferry terminal. *5 rooms | Vrh Lučac 16 | tel. 021 48 27 15 | www.villaana-split.hr | Budget*

## BOAT CONNECTIONS

Regional ferries depart from Split to the islands of *Brač, Hvar, Korčula, Lastovo, Vis* and *Šolta*. The coastal line connects Split with *Rijeka* and *Dubrovnik on a daily basis;* and during the season there is a ferry between *Split–Ancona* three times per week.

## INFORMATION

### TOURIST INFO SPLIT
*Peristil b.b. | tel. 021 34 56 06 | www. visitsplit.com*

concerts. Information is available from the tourist infos or at *www.hnk-split.hr.*

## WHERE TO STAY

### KAŠTEL ☼
This friendly and welcoming B&B in the old town rents out rooms, apartments and a luxury suite, all of which have wonderful views of the Riva. *8 rooms, 2 apartments, 1 suite | Mihovilova širina 5 | tel. 091 120 03 48 | www.kastelsplit.com | Budget–Moderate*

### LE MERIDIEN LAV
The 381 rooms of this new luxury hotel on the beach, 8 km (5 mi) south of Split, are distributed over four buildings in one

## WHERE TO GO

### KAŠTELA – ROUTE OF THE CASTLES
(132 C3) (*ⅉ G–H5*)
The road running parallel to the Adriatic Highway between Split and Trogir connects seven seaside castles, situated on the slopes of the Kozjak Mountains: *Sućurac, Gomilica, Kambelovac, Lukšić, Stari, Novi* and *Štafilić*. A small town has grown around every one. These forts were built by noble families around 500 years ago, to provide protection from Turks and pirates. The most beautiful is that of the Benedictine nuns, *Kaštel Go-*

*milica,* built on a rock in the sea.

The grapes of the exquisite 'Kaštelanski Crljenak' wine grow in the fertile hinterland. A lot of fruit and vegetables are also grown here, and cherries in particular. A cosy konoba can be found by the harbour basin of *Kaštel Novi: Sv. Jure* serves Dalmatian specialities such as *scampi buzara* and the fish stew *brodet.* You can also spend the night here in comfortable rooms *(7 rooms | tel. 021 23 27 59 | Budget).* Information: *Tourist Info Kaštela | Dvorac Vitturi | Brce 1 | Kaštel Lukšić | tel. 021 22 83 55 | www.kastela-info.hr*

### SINJ (132 D2) (*M H4*)

The 35 km (21.7 mi) stretch from Split to Sinj answers the question of what may lie behind the magnificent coastal mountains. The Zagora, a rocky karst landscape, where only the valleys contain fertile soil, begins beyond Klis. At the edge of the wide, level Sinjsko polje, through which the Cetina River flows, is Sinj (population: 4500), which was a constant cause of battles with the Turks and the Venetians. The most recent attempt at conquest was made in 1715, when the Venetians, supported by an army of peasants, won the fight. Since then Sinj has celebrated *Sinjska alka* every year during the first weekend in August. During this knightly tournament everyone gets dressed up in original costumes and uniforms.

### ŠOLTA (132 B–C 3–4) (*M G5*)

Šolta (57 sq km, 22 sq mi, population: 1500) is only 15 km (9.3 mi) from the mainland. The contrast between the lively port of Split and the rural idyll of this 19 km (11.8 mi) long island and its eight tiny villages could not be greater. During summer weekends the city dwellers come in large numbers to go swimming here. The rocky bays on the island's northern side can be reached by car; those on the southern side are only accessible by sea. Most of the holidaymakers stay in apartments and private holiday homes or they book luxury stays in the palace: the 17th-century property in Maslinica, owned by the Marchis, a noble family, is now the exquisite *Hotel Martinis Marchi,* and also features an elegant, highly praised restaurant *(6 rooms | tel. 021 57 27 68 | www.martinis-marchi.com | Expensive).* The villages of *Grohote, Maslenica* and *Stomorska* are

# IVAN MEŠTROVIĆ

You will come across ● Ivan Meštrović's (1883–1962) works a lot during your journey through Dalmatia. In Split you will find the monument for Bishop Gregory of Nin on the northern wall of Diocletian's Palace, in Šibenik there is the one for Juraj Dalmatinac in front of the cathedral. In Cavtat Meštrović even built an entire mausoleum for the Račić shipping family. His major work reflects very different trends in the visual arts. This can also be seen in the sculptor's former summer villa in Split, the *Galerija Meštrović,* where an extensive collection of his works is on display in the house and garden. *Tue–Sun 9am–7pm, in winter Tue–Sat 9am–4pm, Sun 10am–3pm | 30 kunas | Šetaliste Ivana Meštrovića 46*

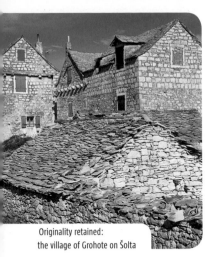

Originality retained:
the village of Grohote on Šolta

the larger, but still very tranquil centres of the island community. The car ferry and hydrofoil depart several times a day from *Split. Information: Tourist Info | Grohote | tel. 021 65 41 51 | www.solta.hr*

# TROGIR

### ▨▨ MAP INSIDE THE
### ▨▨ BACK COVER

(132 B3) *(ΩΩ G5)* **This historic island town (much more than 2000 years old), connected by bridges both to the mainland and to the island of Čiovo, is a treasure trove of art.**

There are churches, palaces and townhouses, Romanesque and Gothic windows, narrow alleys and bright squares, arches and staircases all very close together here. In 1998 historic Trogir (population: 13,000) was declared a Unesco World Heritage Site. Street cafés, shops and restaurants in old buildings keep the town attractive and alive. Along the bridge to Čiovo is the Harbour Gate and a small *Loggia.* The gate leads into the narrow

*Gradska*, that in turn leads on to the main square where the cathedral is to be found.

## SIGHTSEEING

### BENEDICTINE CONVENT (SAMOSTAN SV. NIKOLE XIST)

Right behind the entrance to Gradska, the sacred museum of the Benedictine convent houses a valuable treasure, namely a Greek stone relief from the 3rd century BC. It depicts Kairos, the god of the opportune moment: a winged youth who has a long curl on his forehead, while the back of his head is bare. 'Seizing the moment' is a common figure of speech; it was important enough to the ancient Greeks to give it a deity. *Summer daily 10am–noon, 4pm–6pm | 10 kunas*

### MAIN SQUARE (GRADSKI TRG)/ SV. LOVRO CATHEDRAL ★ ●

The dominant building on the main square is Sv. Lovro cathedral, built between 1200 and 1605: Romanesque elements to Renaissance features, combined to produce a consummate whole. A masterpiece by the great sculptor Radovan is the main portal (13th century), which contains two lions as well as Adam and Eve to the left and right of the cathedral door. Above it a relief depicts saints and hunting scenes as well as plant and animal ornaments. To the left of the portal is the baptistery, which was completed in 1464. Inside the cathedral is the impressive Renaissance chapel of Sv. Ivan Ursini. Climbing up to the ⤴ bell tower will give you lovely views over the roofs of Trogir *(cathedral/tower summer Mon–Sat 9am–7pm | 20 kunas)*. On the eastern side of the main square is the Duke's Palace (now the town hall) with Romanesque arcades and Gothic windows. On the wall you can see the coats of arms of Trogir's noble families. On the southern side the clock tower stands next to the loggia (both 15th century). The judge's stone table dates back to a time when public trials were held in the loggia.

### CITY MUSEUM (GRADSKI MUZEJ)

Opposite the cathedral is the noteworthy Garagnin Baroque palace. It now houses the city museum. The lapidarium in the courtyard also has a relief of the Illyrian deity Silvanus from the 2nd century *July/ Aug daily 9am–9pm, June, Sept daily 9am–noon, 5pm–8pm, otherwise daily 9am–2pm | 15 kunas*

## FOOD & DRINK

### ALKA

Charcoal grilled fish and meat is very tasty. What's special here, however, are the few tables on the intimate, romantic roof terrace. *Augustina Kažotića 15 | tel. 021 88 18 56 | Moderate*

### INSIDER TIP KONOBA PAŠIKE

Opposite Hotel Pašike. Traditional dishes served by staff dressed in traditional Trogir costume. There are also inexpensive dishes of the day. During the summer live acts perform Dalmatian music, but don't worry – it's discreet. *Sinjska | tel. 021 88 51 85 | Moderate*

### TRAGOS

This old town restaurant with its romantic courtyard stands for good fish dishes, which do, however, have their price. *Budislaviceva 3 | tel. 021 88 47 29 | Moderate–Expensive*

View over the roofs of Trogir with its old town centre that's much more than 2000 years old

## SHOPPING

**MARKET**

A few steps behind the Land Gate is the market. Every day the farmers of the surrounding area come here to sell fresh fruit and vegetables. You should definitely try the delicious cherries in early summer.

## WHERE TO STAY

**PAŠIKE**

Stylish rooms with antique furniture in a quiet street in the old town. *7 rooms, 1 apartment | Sinjska | tel. 021 88 51 85 | www.hotelpasike.com | Moderate*

## INFORMATION

**TOURIST INFO**

*Trg Ivana Pavla II/1 | tel. 021 88 56 28 | www.tztrogir.hr*

# VIS

*(132 B5) (🛱 G6)* **The island of Vis (90 sq km, 35 sq mi) is far out in the sea, at the entrance to the Dalmatian archipelago.** The fertile plateau on this mountainous island is cultivated with the vines of the white Vugava grape variety and different vegetables. There are around 4000 islanders, equally divided between the strikingly urban coastal towns of *Vis* and *Komiža*, which are connected by a good road. The old coastal road is much more scenic, but it is also narrow and winding. The ancient Greeks, who called the island Issa, brought the vines, the Venetians the architecture and the British built the fortifications during the Napoleonic era; the Austro-Hungarians built the lighthouses and the first road. In 1944 partisan leader and future prime minister Josip Broz Tito hid from the Germans in

a cave *(Titova špilja)* in the highest mountain, Hum (587 m).

## PLACES ON VIS

**KOMIŽA** (132 B5) *(🛱 G6)*

At the harbour entrance you will find the castle (16th century), now a fishing museum *(June–Sept Mon–Sat 10am–noon, 7pm–10pm, Sun until 10pm | 12 kunas)*, which has on display a typical Vis fishing boat, a *falkuša*. You get a nice view of the town and of the island of Biševo from the �⁂ tower.

In the north of the wide bay of Komiža, in front of which is Biševo island, is *Hotel Biševo (126 rooms | tel. 021 71 31 44 | www.hotel-bisevo.com.hr | Moderate)*, on a pretty pebble beach; it is the only hotel in town. Behind the fish factory, which is closed in summer, there are five further little bathing bays with bubbling fresh water springs.

Not far from the centre, right on the beach, the INSIDER TIP *Konoba Bako* is a surprise with its ancient amphorae, a 5th century anchor and an old wine press *(tel. 021 71 37 42 | Moderate)*. Another original option is the INSIDER TIP *Konoba Jastožera* with its wooden pontoon above the pool of a former lobster farm; fish, lobster and seafood are the mainstays here *(Gundulićeva 6 | tel. 021 71 38 59 | Expensive)*. *Information: Tourist Info | Riva | Komiža | tel. 021 71 34 55 | www.tz-komiza.hr*

**VIS (TOWN)** (132 B5) *(🛱 G6)*

The town of Vis is situated on the northern side of the island, around the sheltered bay of *Viški zaljev*. The park, right next to where the car ferry docks, has seven different palm tree species. Discoveries from ancient Greek times in the *Baterija della Madonna, built by the Austrians and now a museum, give*

Benedictine monks settled in Komiža in the 12th century

an impression of what the old Issa was like (summer Tue–Sun 10am–1pm, 5pm–8pm | 20 kunas | Šetalište Viškš Boj 12 | 20 kunas). At the entrance to the bay are the ruins of the fort built by the British in the early 19th century. ☆ St George's Tower remains extant and is a nice viewpoint from which to take in the sea.

In the old town the small Hotel San Giorgio makes its guests comfortable with 16 pleasant rooms and a good restaurant (Petra Hectorovića 2 | tel. 021 711 3 62 | hotelsangiorgiovis.com | Moderate). In the old quarter, in Kut, there are several konobas. The Pojoda has established a particularly good reputation among gourmets. The chef here is Zoran Brajčić, whose dishes are reminiscent of the old recipes of Vis (Don C. Marasovića 8 | tel. 021 711 5 75 | Expensive).

Vis and the neighbouring Biševo are rich in underwater grottoes – a diverse diving area that also has wrecks in its inventory. Dodoro-Diving offers competently run diving courses and excursions (Kranjcevica 4 | tel. 09 12 51 22 63 | www.dodoro-diving.com). Information: Tourist Info | Šetalište stare Isse 2 | Vis | tel. 021 71 70 17 | www.tz-vis.hr

## BOAT CONNECTION

There is a car ferry between Split–Vis three times a day during the season.

## WHERE TO GO

### BIŠEVO (132 B5) (Ω G7)

Every day small boats depart from Komiža to the island of Biševo, which is only 6 sq km (2.3 sq mi) in size. It is only possible to access the famous ★ ● Blue Grotto (Modra špilja) when the sea is calm. At around noon, the sunlight enters the cave via an opening in the rock located below sea level, transforming the cave into a magnificently colourful place. Biševo has 14 permanent inhabitants as well as some private holiday accommodation. Information: Tourist Info Komiža

# DUBROVNIK REGION

From the Neretva delta to the Bay of Kotor this narrow coastal strip is lined by the karst mountain scenery of the Dinaric Alps. It is a subtropical Mediterranean garden landscape, along the border with Bosnia-Herzegovina and Montenegro.

The focus of the region is the old trading port of Dubrovnik, which over the centuries, until 1808, upheld its status as the Free Republic of Ragusa in the region dominated by the power struggles between the Bosnians, Serbs, Ottomans, Croats and Hungarians. Off the mainland coast are the Pelješac peninsula, the Elaphiti islands Koločep, Lopud and Šipan along with the islands of Korčula, Mljet and Lastovo. Coasts rich in bays, old seafarer towns, excellent winegrowing areas and that other Queen of the Adriatic, Dubrovnik, have presented southern Dalmatia with enormous tourist potential.

## CAVTAT

(135 E6) (*M8*) **The little town occupies a picturesque location on a wooded spit of land at the edge of *Župski zaljev* bay.** Inviting footpaths and extensive pebble beaches mean that every summer all the hotels and guesthouses here are full to the last bed. Cavtat (pop. 1700) is famous for its relaxing holiday opportunities. Along the hotel beaches you will find all sorts of things to do: jet-skiing, banana-boats and tube rides. For divers, there are organized trips to amphorae, wrecks and underwater caves.

Photo: View of Dubrovnik's city walls

## Where Venice came up against its limits: Dubrovnik's cool elegance and enchanting island bays

Even in Antiquity, the town was a flourishing Greco-Roman colony. When the Slavs and Avars stormed the place in the 7th century, the inhabitants fled to a rocky island 17 km (10.6 mi) away – the germ-cell of the ancient city of Ragusa, which later came to be known as Dubrovnik.

### SIGHTSEEING

#### MAUSOLEUM

At the end of the promenade a path with steps leads from the Franciscan priory to the highest point of the peninsula. ☀ In the cemetery is the mausoleum of the Račić shipowning family, designed by the sculptor Ivan Meštrović in 1920–22. *Summer Mon–Sat 9am –12 noon, 4–8pm | 10 kunas*

#### RECTOR'S PALACE (KNEŽEV DVOR)

In the middle of the expansive curve of the seafront promenade is the palace that was formerly the headquarters of the city governors of Dubrovnik. Today the Renaissance building houses the *Municipal Museum* with a graphics col-

Market stalls on Dubrovnik's Gundulićeva poljana

lection comprising 10,000 items (including drawings by Albrecht Dürer) and the valuable library of the lawyer Baltazar Bogišić. *July–Oct Mon–Sat 9am–2pm, otherwise Mon–Fri 9am–2pm | 20 kunas*

## FOOD & DRINK

### KOLONA ☙
From the quiet terrace in the greenery you have a bird's eye view of life in the town. We can recommend the grilled seafood kebabs. *Put Tihe 2 | tel. 020 47 87 87 | Moderate*

### LEUT
A restaurant with a long tradition in the heart of the town on the promenade. Famous for its scampi risotto and for fish cooked under the peka. *Trumbićev put 11 | tel. 020 47 84 77 | Moderate*

## SPORTS & LEISURE

In the surroundings of Cavtat most of the beaches have been straightened with concrete platforms. Diving is a rewarding activity, as expeditions can be made to INSIDER TIP▶ ancient shipwrecks. Excursions are organized by *Diving Center Epidaurum (Šetalište Žal | tel. 020 47 13 86 | www.epidaurum-cavtat-diving.hr).*

## WHERE TO STAY

### CASTALLETTO
Pleasant family boarding-house overlooking the harbour with modern rooms. *14 rooms | Frana Laureana 22 | tel. 020 47 95 47 | www.dubrovnikexperience. com | Moderate*

### LOVAC ☙
This friendly boarding-house is pleasantly situated on the slope above Cavtat with a panoramic view of the bay. *4 rooms, 3 flats | Put od Cavtata 3 | tel. 020 47 84 56 | www.cavtat-pansion-lovac. com | Budget–Moderate*

## INFORMATION

### TOURIST INFO
*Tiha 3 | tel. 020 47 90 25 | www. tzcavtat-konavle.hr*

## WHERE TO GO

### KONAVLE (135 E6) (𝄢 M8)
The Konavle valley, between the sea and a semicircular mountain range, is southern Dalmatia's larder where Croatia meets Bosnia and Montenegro. The main town in Konavle is *Gruda*. From here there is a waymarked path to the restau-

rant *Konavoski dvori* a few kilometres away, romantically situated on the River Ljuta. Waiters in local costume serve regional cuisine, including lamb dishes, trout and fresh bread baked on the premises *(Ljuta | tel. 020 79 10 39 | Moderate)*. Traditional Konavle specialities can also be found in the little konoba *Vinica*, just a few hundred metres away, also on the River Ljuta *(tel. 020 79 12 44 | Budget)*.

Konavle dances are performed in local costume every Sunday at 11.15am after mass in summer by the villagers of *Čilipi*. As this tradition now attracts bus-loads of visitors, the villagers make an admission charge *(35 kunas)*. In spite of the commercialization, this is an entertaining spectacle that's certainly worth seeing. *16 km (9.9 mi) to the south-east*

# DUBROVNIK

**MAP INSIDE THE BACK COVER**
*(135 D5) (∭ L7)* The 'Pearl of the Adriatic', a World Heritage Site at the foot of bare karst slopes. With 50,000 inhabitants Dubrovnik is a pretty sizable place these days.

The part of ancient *Ragusa* (the town has only been known officially as Dubrovnik since 1918) that attracts countless tourists all year round is the old quarter with its imposing fortified wall. It is in this heart of the former Free Maritime Republic – largely independent from the Middle Ages to the start of the 19th century – that the most important sights are concentrated. To the north is what is now the business quarter, which connects the old town with the district of *Gruž* and its harbour and dockyard facilities. Opposite them is the *Lapad peninsula* with its pine forests, the green lung of the city and a popular relaxing seaside holiday resort.

## SIGHTSEEING

### OLD TOWN ★
The harmonious structure of the core of the old town, today, incidentally, **INSIDER TIP** completely equipped with WiFi, and its numerous artworks and historic monuments have made Dubrovnik a centre of Mediterranean World Heritage. Our tour leads first through the *Pile Gate* with the statue of the city's patron saint, Sv. Vlaho (St Blaise), and then left to the *Sv. Spas Chapel of the Redeemer* (16th century) and the *Franciscan Church*. Between the two is a narrow passage leading to the *Franciscan Priory*.

The *Large Onofrio's Fountain* (1438) covered by a shallow dome, which consists

★ **Dubrovnik's old town**
Within the magnificent city walls the memory of the free Republic of Ragusa is alive → p. 81

★ **Botanical Gardens**
The Arboretum in Trsteno is a Renaissance park with Mediterranean and exotic plants and trees → p. 87

★ **Korčula (town)**
Marco Polo was allegedly born in the picturesque alleys of this town → p. 90

★ **Lastovo**
The green island is considered an insider tip for individual Robinson Crusoe holidays → p. 93

★ **Mljet**
The lake with its island on Mljet is an attractive area of countryside → p. 94

**MARCO POLO HIGHLIGHTS**

**CITY WHERE TO START?**
A good starting point for a tour of the city is **Pile Gate** in the west of the old town, where the tourist info is located. From there you have direct access to the historic centre or you can opt for a tour along the city walls. Parking is possible in **Iza Grada** along the northern city walls. There are buses to Pile Gate from the bus station *(Obala pape Ivana -Pavla II 44 A in Gruž)*.

of 16 individual fountains, is a popular rendezvous both for tourists and the local youth. This is the starting point of the *Placa*, also known as the *Stradun*, the city's promenade where people go to see and be seen. It leads across the former Maritime Canal, now filled in, which used to divide the two settlements of Ragusa and Dubrava. The simple rows of natural-stone houses, devoid of balconies, were build on the foundations of the ruined palaces on either side of the Placa following the earthquake of 1667. The street ends on *Luža Square*, with its prestige buildings. It contains the *Small Onofrio's Fountain* and the *Roland Column* (1418), symbolizing market and trade privileges in the Middle Ages. The Baroque façade belongs to the church of *Sv. Vlaho* (18th century); opposite is the *Sponza Palace* (16th century). Along the short side of the square are, from left to right, the municipal *Bell Tower* (15th century), the Neo-gothic building (19th century) with the *Theatre* and the *Municipal Café* and the *Rector's Palace*. A few yards further on is the impressive cathedral of *Velika Gospa*.

## CITY WALL (GRADSKE ZIDINE) ⚓

A bird's eye view of Dubrovnik and a long view out to sea: the effect is most spectacular from the late afternoon, when the tiled roofs of the old town, which is laid out on a grid pattern, glow in the warm red hue of the rays of the setting sun. *Summer daily 9am–7.30 pm, winter 10am–3 pm | 70 kunas*

## FRANCISCAN PRIORY (FRANJEVAČKI SAMOSTAN)

The courtyard of the 14th-century priory, situated near Pile Gate, is surrounded by a cloister supported on filigree columns. At this cloister is a pharmacy that was founded in 1317 and still survives in its original condition, making it one of the oldest in Europe; there is also a library. *Summer daily 9am–6pm, winter 9am–5pm | 25 kunas*

## RECTOR'S PALACE (KNEŽEV DVOR)

In complete isolation from his family and the outside world, one of the city's noblemen would run the republic's government business from here, but each one only for a month at a time. Quite in the spirit of Dubrovnik, this 15th century palace is characterized by a harmonious beauty that does not rely on excessive grandiosity. The city museum it houses today documents what life was once like in the republic: on display are weapons, clothes, furniture, paintings and the keys to the city gates. *Summer daily 9am–6pm, winter Mon–Sat 9am–2pm | 40 kunas*

## SPONZA PALACE

The late-Gothic and Renaissance styles complement each other wonderfully in this 16th century building. Merchants brought their trading goods from all over the world to this palace, which was used as the customs house.

## SYNAGOGUE

Dubrovnik possessed a large Jewish community, whose synagogue is one of the oldest in the Balkans. The simple place of worship is hidden on the second floor of a Gothic townhouse. *Summer daily 10am–8pm, winter Mon–Fri 9am–noon | Žudioska ul. 5 | 15 kunas*

### SV. VLAHO
This Baroque church (18th century) has a particular treasure on its main altar, namely a silver-gilt statue of the city's patron saint Sv. Vlaho (St Blaise).

### VELIKA GOSPA (ASSUMPTION)
The cathedral's monumental interior (17th century) houses valuable paintings, including a work by Titian at the main altar, the *Assumption*. Among the 138 relics in the rich treasure chamber, there is also the skull of Sv. Vlaho, mounted in the shape of a Byzantine crown. *Summer Mon–Sat 9am–5pm, Sun 11am–5pm, winter Mon–Sat 10am–noon, 3pm–5pm, Sun 11am–noon, 3pm–5pm | 15 kunas*

### VISIA DUBROVNIK 5D THEATRUM ●
5D animation with vibrating seats and wind effects take visitors on a journey through Dubrovnik's history, from the city's founding to its siege by the Yugoslav army. *Daily 9am–10pm | Poljana Paska Milicevica 4 | 75 kunas | www.visi adubrovnik.com*

## FOOD & DRINK

Parallel to the central Placa is *Prijeko*, a street with vine-covered façades, where you will find a whole number of restaurants.

### INSIDER TIP ▶ BUFFET KAMENICE
This cosy eatery is a popular meeting place with the locals in the evenings. You will be served small servings, risottos and omelettes as well as fresh oysters. *Gundulićeva poljana 8 | tel. 020 42 14 99 | Moderate*

### BUFFET ŠKOLA
Fast food Croatian style at very inexpensive prices. All of the dishes are good and tastily prepared. The restaurant is located in a former school. *Antuninska 1 | tel. 020 32 10 96 | Budget*

Old harbour of Dubrovnik, Europe's best-preserved fortified city

### GIL'S CUISINE & POP LOUNGE
A high flier: a modern interior with a perfect location within historic walls, not far from the old harbour; fusion cuisine prepared by a master of his craft and a purple lounge, ideal for relaxing. *Svetog Dominika | tel. 020 32 22 21 | Moderate*

### GRADSKAVANA
Newly furnished with a bright interior, this café remains the afternoon meeting place for Dubrovnik's intellectuals. *Pred Dvorom | tel. 020 32 10 65 | Budget*

### LOKANDA PESKARIJA
This rustic konoba is situated in the old harbour, right behind the Rector's Palace. Simple, fresh fish dishes, well prepared and inexpensive. *Na Ponti | tel. 020 32 47 50 | Budget*

### MEA CULPA
In a somewhat hidden location in a back street parallel to the Placa, this pizzeria serves huge pizzas and pasta dishes. *Za rokom 3 | tel. 020 32 34 30 | Moderate*

### PROTO
Elegant fish restaurant with a huge roof terrace in the middle of the old town. *Široka 1 | tel. 020 32 32 34 | Expensive*

### SESAME
The cuisine here blends Dalmatian and Mediterranean influences; lots of salad, vegetables and a large selection of fish and meat. *Dante Alighieria b.b. | tel. 020 41 29 10 | www.sesame.hr | Moderate–Expensive*

## SHOPPING

The main road, *Stradun*, is lined by souvenir shops and bookshops.

### DUBROVAČKA KUĆA
Comprehensive selection of good quality regional souvenirs. *Svetog Dominika bb*

# THE WOUNDS BEHIND THE FAÇADE

After the Croats had voted for their country's independence in a referendum, the troops of what remained of Yugoslavia started their siege of Dubrovnik in June 1991. The city became completely isolated; electricity, gas and water became scarce. Shelling during the nine-month siege damaged or destroyed 68 percent of the historic buildings in the old town. The military campaign reached its climax on 6 December 1991, when 600 shells fell on the city in a single day. It was not until the spring of 1992 that the Croatian army managed to liberate Dubrovnik.

Today there is not much to remind people of the wounds of those days. The houses have been restored, the tiled roofs repaired and the immaculate beauty of the city revived, as if nothing had ever happened. Only the museum opened on the mountain of Srd in 2010 deals with the siege and the Croatian War of Independence. *Summer daily 9am–6pm, winter daily 9am–4pm | 20 kunas*

The ☺ *Deša* initiative also looks after the psychological wounds of the many traumatized women by running projects that support their financial independence. *Deša | Frana Supila 8 | www.desa-dubrovnik.hr*

The Placa, also known as Stradun, now crosses the old town where a canal was once located

## NATURAL COSMETICS ☺

The cosmetics sold in the pharmacy of the Franciscan priory are made using old recipes and natural ingredients such as roses, almonds and honey.

### BEACHES

For a quick dip the rocks behind a gap in the city walls in the alley called ● Od Margarite suffice. But for a day at the beach it is better to use Dubrovnik's city beach Banje (sand/pebbles) to the south of the old town, where the East-West-Beachclub has established itself with elegant loungers, a restaurant and a lounge (www.ew-dubrovnik.com). On the island of Lokrum there are many small rock and pebble bays where you can go swimming with a view of the old town. There are also lovely pebble bays and beaches all around Lapad peninsula.

## INSIDER TIP SEA KAYAKING ☺

Half-day excursions in kayaks to the island of Lokrum and around the old town with information and wildlife and the environment are organized by *Adria Adventure (ca. 270 kunas | tel. 020 33 25 67 | www.adriaadventure.hr)*.

### ENTERTAINMENT

Galleries and studios are open until late at night. During the summer there will always be a play, a concert or a folklore performance in the Lazareti. The evening begins here with a drink at sunset by the city wall in Rivelin Club *(Sv. Dominika bb)*. The cosy music bar INSIDER TIP *Troubadour* opposite the Rector's Palace has live jazz and blues performances. The in-crowd meet in the INSIDER TIP *East-West-Beachclub* on Banje beach, which is frequented by popular DJs *(www.ew-dubrovnik.com)*.

# DUBROVNIK

## WHERE TO STAY

The prices charged by hotels in Dubrovnik are significantly above the Croatian average. Many people living in Dubrovnik rent out rooms or apartments, which is a cheaper alternative to the hotels. Two spacious apartments in the old town are available from *Vesna Miletić* for example *(Poljana Mrtvo Zvono 1 | tel. 020 43 63 06 | www.villa-vesna.com | Budget).* The *Ivušić family* has two rooms and an ☆ apartment with stunning views of the old town *(2 rooms, 1 apartment | Bernarda Shawa 1 | tel. 020 43 26 54 | www. apartmani-ivusic.hr | Budget).*

### BELLEVUE ☆
This elegant oasis of tranquillity close to the old town has views of the cliffs and the sea as well as a lift down to the small, public bathing bay *91 rooms | Pera Cingrije 7 | tel. 020 33 00 00 | www. hotel-bellevue.hr | Expensive*

### DUBROVNIK OH
This youth hostel is only a ten-minute walk above the old town. Guests (no age limit) must have a Hostelling International membership card. 19 basic, clean 4 and 6-bed dorms. *Vinka Sagrestana 3 | tel. 020 42 32 41 | www.hfhs. hr | Budget*

### STARI GRAD
Pretty little old town hotel in a heritage building. ☆ The views from the roof terrace are outstanding. *8 rooms | Od Sigurate 4 | tel. 020 32 22 44 | www. hotelstarigrad.com | Expensive*

### VILA MICIKA
Family-run guesthouse above Lapad Bay, basic but well furnished and inexpensive compared with other options in Dubrovnik. *7 rooms | Mata Vodopica 10 |* *tel. 020 43 73 32 | www.vilamicika.hr | Moderate–Expensive*

## INFORMATION

**TOURIST INFO**
*Pile | Brsalje 5 | tel. 020 31 20 11 | www. tzdubrovnik.hr*

## WHERE TO GO

**LOKRUM** (135 D5) *(𝄞 L8)*
There are boats that go to the small, green island (80 hectares) with its bathing bays; they depart from Dubrovnik's harbour at the eastern entrance (Pločetor) to the old town. In 1859 the Austrian Archduke Maximilian bought the island, built a palace on it, refurbished the Benedictine monastery and created the beautiful park with its subtropical plants. In the small, shallow saltwater lake Mrtvo more (Dead Sea) children and those who cannot swim can splash around safely. *5-minute trip | 40 kunas*

## NERETVA DELTA/PLOČE
### (134 B–C4) (*⊞ K6*)

Between *Neum* and *Ploče* the coastal mountains open up, leaving room for the 280 km (174 mi) Neretva, whose water spreads out to form a wide delta where the river flows into the Adriatic. Parts of this former marshland were drained to allow the cultivation of fruit and vegetables. The area that was left untouched is used as a breeding spot for many different water birds. Migratory birds come to rest at the richly laid table. The river arms are rich in fish and are the domain of eels and carp. The delta's main town is *Metković*, prettily situated on the *Neretva*. Your accommodation option on the delta is the hotel and restaurant Villa Neretva (tel. 020 67 22 00 | www.hotel-villa-ner etva.com | *Moderate*), which has eight friendly rooms. The restaurant's speciality is eel dishes.

### INSIDER TIP SRD ⛷ (135 D5) (*⊞ L7*)

Dubrovnik's 412 m (450 yd) local mountain has the best views of the old town and the sea. During the Yugoslav War it became the symbol of Croatian defence. In the fort built under Napoleon, Croatian soldiers defended Dubrovnik against the Yugoslav besiegers. The old cableway was destroyed at the time and it was only replaced by a new one in 2010. The panorama remains outstanding. Anyone interested in the Croatian war of independence will find in-depth information and footage in the museum (see box p. 84). *Cableway daily 9am–9pm | Trip up and down 75 kunas | www. dubrovnikcablecar.com*

### TRSTENO (135 D5) (*⊞ L7*)

In Trsteno, 18 km (11.2 mi) north of Dubrovnik, the lovely ★ *Botanical Gardens (Arboretum | May–Oct daily 8am–7pm, Nov–April 8am–5pm | 25 kunas)* are worth visiting. They feature Mediterranean and exotic trees, bushes and flowers. The 3-hectare Renaissance park around the palace villa was created in the early 16th century by the patrician Gučetić-Gozze family from Dubrovnik

The fertile Neretva delta is the life blood of southern Dalmatia and navigable by small boats

# ELAPHITI ISLANDS

● **(135 D5)** *(฿ L7)* **The 13 Elaphiti Islands are situated off the mainland coast between Dubrovnik and Pelješac (Deer Islands).**

smallest of the Elaphiti Islands. Its two villages, *Gornje Čelo* and *Donje Čelo*, are connected via a footpath. When walking from one village to the other (approx. 20 mins), you can discover gardens with orange and lemon trees, carob trees and olive groves as well as the ruins of a medieval fort. Fragments of Roman sculptures and some early medieval Croatian

One destination of many visitors to Dubrovnik is the smallest of the Elaphiti Islands: Koločep

The three inhabited Elaphiti islands, which are covered in subtropical vegetation, are *Šipan, Lopud* and *Koločep* (together population: 1000). They are a popular and largely car-free destination with many nice bathing beaches. The Elaphiti Islands, which were colonized by the ancient Greeks, were part of the Republic of Ragusa. In the 15th and 16th centuries merchants and the clergy built themselves generous summer residences on these small natural paradises.

### KOLOČEP (135 D5) *(฿ L7)*
At just 2.4 sq km (1 sq mi) Koločep is the

wattle can be found on the walls of *Sv. Marija* (13th century), the parish church of Donje Čelo.

### LOPUD (135 D5) *(฿ L7)*
The island of Lopud covers 4.6 sq km (1.8 sq mi). Since there are freshwater springs here, agaves, palm trees, cypresses and lemon and orange trees flourish. The island's only town is Lopud, which stretches out in a large arc around a pebbly bay all the way to the ruins of the former Franciscan priory. Cosy cafés and taverns as well as the former summer residences of the business merchants

from Ragusa are situated on the pretty waterfront promenade. On the island's east coast, an approximately 20-minute walk from the town of Lopud, you will find the idyllic bay of *Šuruj,* which boasts fine, golden sand. The `INSIDER TIP` *Villa Vilina* is a small, elegant family-run hotel with a good restaurant *(14 rooms, 3 apartments | tel. 020 75 93 33 | www.villa-vilina.hr | Expensive)*. A more basic option, run by a committed young couple, is *La Villa (6 rooms | Obala Iva Kuljevana 5 | tel. 091 3 22 01 26 | www.lavilla.com.hr | Moderate)*.

## ŠIPAN (135 D5) (*∅ L7*)

At 16.5 sq km (6.4 sq mi), Šipan is the largest island in the Elaphiti archipelago. Wine is also grown here. The island's main town is *Šipanska Luka.* Its Rector's Palace (15th century), once the seat of Ragusa's governor, is situated above the town and is evidence of its former glory. Modern pleasures can be satisfied in the highly praised restaurant *Kod Marka (at the Mole | tel. 020 75 80 07 | Expensive)*. A walk (1 hour) on the car-free island will take you from Šipanska Luka to the fishing village of *Sudjuradj,* where you will find the restored Renaissance villa of the noble Stjepović-Skočibuha family (15th century). If you have fallen in love with this place, you will find a stylish place to stay in *Hotel Božica.* It also has a good restaurant with views of the sea *(26 rooms | tel. 020 32 54 00 | www.hotel-bozica.hr | Expensive)*. The trail leads past the remains of the former summer residence of the bishops of Ragusa, built in the 16th century.

## BOAT CONNECTION

During the main season there is a passenger ferry that plies between *Dubrovnik–Koločep–Lopud–Šipan* four times a day.

## INFORMATION

**TOURIST INFO**
Vukovarska *24 | Dubrovnik | tel. 020 32 49 99 | www.visitdubrovnik.hr*

# KORČULA

(133 D–E5–6) (*∅ H–J7*) **The island of Korčula (population: 17,000) covers 276 sq km (107 sq mi), making it one of Dalmatia's largest islands. Thanks to its black-green pines, stone pines and the evergreen holm oaks, which cover more than half of the island, its ancient name was Korkyra melaina (Black Island).**
Its fertile valleys are used to grow olives, fruit and vegetables. Excellent local wines, such as Grk, Pošip, Rukatac and the fiery red Plavac, grow in sunny vineyards on gently sloping hills.

## LOW BUDGET

▶ The *Express Restaurant* is self-service. The food is adequate and significantly cheaper than in the other restaurants in Dubrovnik. *Ul. M. Kaboge 1*

▶ Pizza, pasta and salads are particularly inexpensive in the friendly bistro *Buffet Atlas* at Cavtat's harbour.

▶ A cheap bed, partying and meeting other travellers – Korčula's *Onelove Hostel* is the right place for that. *65 beds | Hrvatske Bratske Zajednice 6 | tel. 020 716755, mobile 098 9 976353 | www.korculabackpacker.com*

From 1427 to 1797 Venice's rule here was unbroken, side by side with its rival, Ragusa, whose territory also included Pelješac peninsula on the other side of *Pelješki channel*, which, at its narrowest, is only 1.3 km (0.8 mi) wide. For a long time the people of Korčula were farmers and fishermen. In contrast to most of the other inhabitants of Dalmatia's island world, they were also hardworking craftsmen, boat-builders and seafarers. As a result Korčula is far less affected by young people moving away than is the case on other islands. In recent decades tourism has become the most important source of income.

The island is accessible via ferry. They dock at the harbour of *Vela Luka* on the western side of the island and at the picturesque town of *Korčula*. The wide road through the mountainous interior (45 km, 28 mi) connects the two towns.

## PLACES ON KORČULA

### BLATO (133 D5) *(₥ H7)*

At the edge of the fertile valley of Blatsko polje is the town of Blato (population: 4000), the centre of the island's agricultural products. The town is also known for its winery. The old loggia stands next to the parish church of Svi Sveti (14th century). The knight tournament 'Kumpanija' is performed every year on the main square on 28 April (Day of Sv. Vizenza, patron saint of Blato). There is a 1 km (0.6 mi) lime-tree avenue that runs through the centre of town. Information: *Tourist Info | Trg F. Tudjmana 4 | Blato | tel. 020 85 18 50 | www.tzo-blato.hr*

### KORČULA (TOWN) ★ ● (133 E5) *(₥ J7)*

The picturesque medieval old town, built on a headland and surrounded by fortified town walls, ought to be viewed from the water too. The foot passenger ferry from the town of Orebić, opposite, docks right outside the town gate.

According to an island legend, the famous Asia traveller Marco Polo (1254–1324), who dictated his adventures to a fellow inmate while in Genoese captivity, was born in Korčula. In a small side street near the cathedral is the Marco Polo House, which has been closed for years now as it is at risk of falling down. There are plans to convert it into a museum. The tower is open to visitors during the summer months *(daily 10am–1pm, 5pm–7pm | 12 kunas)*.

The old town was planned. Branching off from the dead straight main road, on which the most important sights are located, there are narrow alleys, whose rows of houses shelter each other against the sun and the wind. The main entrance is the Land Gate, which can be reached by the monumental neo-Baroque stone stairs at the edge of a small market square. Walk through the gate to get to the square called *Braća Radić*. On the left-hand side is the town hall (16th century), with arcades supported by attractive columns, as well as the Chapel of Our Lady of the Snows, built in memory of the defeat of the Turkish fleet in 1571. A few steps up, the street widens to become the cathedral square, on which the two most beautiful patrician palaces of the city, Arneri and Gabrielis, stand opposite the cathedral of Sv. Marko and the bishop's palace with the treasure chamber.

The large cathedral, Gothic and Renaissance in style, was built in the 15th and 16th centuries using the white stone from Korčula. Two lions adorn the main portal. The main altar features a painting by the Venetian master Tintoretto. It depicts the patron saints of Korčula and Dalmatia: St Mark, St Jerome and St Bartholomew, who is also the patrol saint

Particularly attractive from the water: the old town of Korčula on the island of the same name

of boat-builders. Valuable sacred objects and paintings from the cathedral are on display in the bishop's palace *(July/Aug daily 10am–noon, 5pm–7pm, otherwise after advance reservation | 20 kunas)*.

The city museum in the Gabrielis palace (16th century) possesses a lapidarium with Greek inscriptions; they are documents of the Greek colonization of the original Illyrian population. The upper floors focus on the long tradition of boat-building, seafaring and craftsmanship *(summer daily 10am–9pm, winter Mon–Fri 10am–2pm | 15 kunas)*.

The medieval sword dance 'Moreška' has been a tradition in Korčula for almost 400 years; it is regularly performed in the old town during the summer months. A sight that is almost an invitation to mystic contemplation is the 101-step staircase up to ☙ **INSIDERTIP** the chapel of *Sv. Antun* (St Anthony), lined by cypress espaliers. This is a peaceful spot from which to enjoy the views of the areas around the town of Korčula. Branching off from the street towards Lumbarda

are the steps that lead to the Sv. Antun neighbourhood.

The town of Korčula (population: 3200) is not just a place to go sightseeing. It is also a holiday destination. Adjoining the old town walls is the nostalgic Korčula hotel, with its vine-covered terrace and good cuisine *(20 rooms | tel. 020 71 10 78 | www.hotelkorcula.com | Moderate)*. From restaurants to pizzerias, there are plenty of places in the town centre looking after your wellbeing. The freshest fish is served at *Kanavelić at reasonable prices (Ul. Sv. Barbare 12 | tel. 020 71 18 00 | Moderate)*. The bar Massimo, located high up in the defensive tower Zakerjan *(Setalište petra Kanavelića)* is a romantic spot to have an aperitif.

There are three konobas somewhat outside of the centre that serve the typical dishes of the island. If you order in advance, ☺ *Hajduk* will serve you gently cooked goat's meat, prepared under a peka, accompanied by home-grown vegetables *(8 rooms | Sv. Anton | tel. 020 71 12 67 | Budget)*. *Pogača*, deep-fried dough with a topping of your choice, or octopus cooked under a peka are available in the konoba *Maslina (Lumbarajska cesta | tel. 020 711720 | Budget–Moderate)*. 'Everything organic' is the promise in ☺ INSIDER TIP *Agriturismo Mate*, where you will be treated to delicious Dalmatian cuisine using home-reared meat and home-grown vegetables as well as aromatic herbal drinks *(Pupnat | 13 km (8.1 mi) east of the town of Korčula | tel. 020 7158 67 | Moderate)*.

Korčula's town beaches *Banje* (pebbles) and Luca *Korčulanska* (sand) tend to get very busy during the summer months. There is an absolute dream bay (pebbles) near *Pupnatska Luka,* 15 km (9.3 mi) west of Korčula. Information: *Tourist Info | Obala V. Paletina | Korčula | tel. 020 7157 01 | www.visitkorcula.com*

### LUMBARDA (133 E5–6) (*𝄂 J7*)

Natural sandy beaches, a real trump for tourism: Lumbarda (population: 1100) has them, because the entire eastern tip of the island has a sandy soil that gives the local golden yellow wine, Grk, its special bouquet. Lumbarda's centre, 8 km (5 mi) from the town of Korčula, stretches around the shallow bay of *Prvižal*, where fishing boats and yachts bob up and down. A few Renaissance villas reveal that this spot has long been a popular summer destination.

Leave the centre via the mulberry avenue (uphill) and make your way through Lumbarda's fields and vineyards, to get to the sandy bays of *Pržina* and *Bili Žal*. There is plenty of private accommodation in holiday homes and guesthouses both in and around Lumbarda. The ☺ farm of *Frano Milina Bire* is particularly recommendable. As an organic farmer he was the first on Korčula to be selected for EU subsidies; the white wine (Grk) he grows using traditional methods has won awards *(10 rooms | tel. 020 7120 07 | free-du.t-com. hr/mmbire | Budget)*.

Divers will find competent teachers certified through CMAS and PADI as well as guides for underwater excursions at *MM-Sub*; the diving school also lets apartments *(3 apartments | Tatinja 65 | tel. 020 7123 21 | www.mm-sub.hr | Budget)*.

# MOREŠKA

The traditional sword dance, which originated in Spain, used to be popular all over the Mediterranean. In Korčula the Moreška has firmly held on to its place in the local customs for the past 400 years. The story is about Moro, the son of the Arab emperor Otmanović, who kidnaps the fiancée (bula = Muslim woman) of the white king Osman. The sword dance is meant to decide who will be permitted to marry her. In the final scene the black knights are defeated and Moro hands over his sword and the bula to the victor as a symbol of his submission. Originally the Moreška symbolized the Spanish victory over the Moors, the Christian victory over the Muslims. Today it stands for the victory of love and of good over evil. *June–mid-October at least one performance per week in Korčula's open-air cinema and small free performances on Korčula's town square as well as in other locations on the island*

Information: *Tourist Info | Lumbarda | tel. 020 71 20 05 | www.lumbarda.hr*

### VELA LUKA (133 D5) *(Ø H7)*

The largest town on the island is on Korčula's western side, at the innermost point of a deep bay with several nice pebble beaches. The town centre of the bustling Vela Luka (population: 4450) is

## WHERE TO GO

### LASTOVO ★ (134 A5) *(Ø H–J7)*

To the south of Korčula and at the far edge of the Dalmatian archipelago, the island of Lastovo (53 sq km, 20 sq mi; population: 1250) remains almost undiscovered. The green forests and fertile fields suggest that this place is rich in

Lastovo, once a military restricted area, is still largely untouched by tourism

home to the neo-Baroque parish church of Sv. Josip (19th century), in front of which is a lovely drinking-water well dating from 1930. There are a few cafés, taverns and bistros along the small harbour basin, including the relaxed pizzeria and bar *Casablanca (Moderate)*. The ferries to the island of Lastovo and to Split dock to the south of the harbour basin near the industrial quarter. *Information: Tourist Info | Ulica 41 br. 11 | Vela Luka | tel. 020 81 36 19 | www.tzvelaluka.hr*

## BOAT CONNECTIONS

The coastal line between Rijeka–Dubrovnik departs every day from the town of Korčula; there are also daily departures to *Orebić/Pelješac*, as well as to *Ubli/Lastovo–Vela Luka–Hvar–Split.*

water, even though there is not a single freshwater spring on the entire island. Any moisture here comes from the little bit of rain and the heavy dews formed during the night. Only few hikers and passionate divers explore the harsh beauty of this island of tranquillity, which only has a few swimming beaches, but is all the more blessed with hiking trails and underwater diving areas.

*The town of Lastovo* is attractive; the houses are built up a slope and their chimneys resemble minarets. The Renaissance church of Sv. Kuzma i Damjan has an excellent baptismal font; the loggia opposite is also worth going to see.

As things stand there is only private accommodation on the island as well as in the beach hotel *Solitudo* in *Pasadur,* a friendly place that also has a professionally run diving school *(114 rooms | tel. 020 80 21 00 | www.diving-paradise.net | Moderate)*. Even more solitude is guaranteed by the basic apartments in the lighthouse of *Struga (www.lighthouses-croatia.com | Budget)*. The konoba *Triton (Zaklopatica | tel. 020 80 11 61 | Moderate)* always serves freshly caught fish and is a popular spot with sailors.

The *Tourist Info* in the town of Lastovo *(only open during the peak season | tel. 020 80 10 18)* has information about the hiking trails on this island that has been declared a nature park. *Daily car ferry and catamaran from Vela Luka, 1.5 hrs and 45 mins respectively*

# MLJET

★ *(134 B–C5) (Ⅶ K7)* **Those who choose Mljet (population: 1250) as their holiday destination should know what to expect on this 100 sq km (38.6 sq mi), mountainous island: virtually nothing but untamed nature and cultivated landscape, in among which small villages, overlooked by the restless zeitgeist, are tucked away.**

No promenades, no shopping streets, no fashionable bars and definitely no debauched nightlife. The 'island on the island', that's the island in the larger of the two salt lakes on which the Benedictines built a monastery in the early 12th century, is a popular destination. Both lakes are now part of Mljet National Park *(entry fee 100 kunas, to be paid in Pomena or Polače)*. From the bay of Pomena, where you will usually see a few yachts, there is a trail through the pine forest to the jetty for the boats that cross over to the *monastery island of Sv. Marija*. The Benedictine abbey was once a very defensive structure, featuring a defensive tower and arrow slits. Now it has *Melita,* a romantically situated restaurant *(Veliko jezero | tel. 020 74 41 45| Moderate)*.

A shoreline trail runs around the lakes, romantically framed by forested mountains, and there is also a surfaced road, but it is closed to vehicles from May

Pure nature: canoes on Lake Malo jezero on the mountainous island of Mljet

to October. On its eastern side, at the bridge of Veliki most, the *Veliko jezero* is connected to the open sea via the narrow *Solinski kanal*. Between the small lake *Malo jezero* and the larger lake *Veliko jezero* you can hire canoes, kayaks and bicycles. This is also where you will find Mljet's eco-hotel ☺ *Soline 6,* which aims to have as little impact on the environment of the national park as possible and to that end has solar heating, a biocomposting facility, passive cooling and a grey-water treatment facility *(4 studios | tel. 020 74 40 24 | www.soline6.com | Moderate).*

The harbour of *Polače* with the remains of an ancient Roman palace and the ruins of an early Christian basilica (5th century) is also part of the national park. From here the main road across the island winds its way through the karst mountains, around rugged cliff faces and past fertile valleys in which vegetables and wine are cultivated.

*Odisejeva špilja* can be reached on foot from the elongated ribbon village of *Babino Polje*, the largest settlement on the island. At noon the light in this sea grotto is at its most beautiful. Maybe it is really the place where the nymph Calypso fell in love with the hero Odysseus, as claimed by the Greek poet Homer. The idyllically situated bay of *Sobra,* which has a ferry terminal, and the sandy bay of *Saplunara* in the east of the island are also both well worth visiting.

The coastal line between *Rijeka–Dubrovnik* always docks in *Sobra/Mljet* on Wednesdays. The car ferry *Dubrovnik–Sobra/Mljet* runs twice a day during the peak season.

## INFORMATION

**NACIONALNI PARK MLJET**
*Govedari Pristanište 2 | Mljet | tel. 020 74 40 41 | www.mljet.hr*

# PELJEŠAC

(134 A–C 4–5) (*ℳ J–K 6–7*) **Seafaring and wine made Pelješac peninsula (population: 8000) famous; it is known as the 'island of captains' and as the home of Croatia's best red wines. It stretches out for 65 km (40 mi) between the mainland and the islands of Korčula and Mljet.** Near *Ston*, at the narrowest spot along the isthmus to Pelješac, a powerful fortified wall is a reminder of the period between 1333 and 1808, when the peninsula was part of the Republic of Ragusa and played an important defensive role as an outpost. The bathing spots are all on the south coast, beneath the island's mountains that are largely covered in maquis. Subtropical fruits flourish in the island's valleys meanwhile.

## PLACES ON PELJEŠAC

**DONJA BANDA, PRIZDRINA, POTOMJE (WINE VILLAGES)** (134 B–C4) (*ℳ K7*)
Dingač, Postup and Plavac are the red wines that are produced on Pelješac peninsula, using the grapes of the Plavac mali variety. They are grown between Orebić and Ston. Postup grows beyond Orebić. It bears the name of the coastal village 6 km (3.7 mi) away. The large winery Postup is in the village of Donja Banda, which lies on the island's winding main road. 2 km (1.2 mi) further there is a road branching off into the small old village of Prizdrina. When visiting the private INSIDER TIP▸ winemaker Bartulović *(tel. 020 74 23 46 | www.vinarijabartu*

*lovic.hr*) you should not just try the Plavac Bartul, but also the rosé, which is not commonly produced in Dalmatia.

After three further kilometres you will reach INSIDER**TIP** Potomje, the centre of the top-quality wine *dingač.* A low tunnel leads from the village to the steep southern cliffs above the sea. The grapes spend the whole day ripening in the sunlight that is reflected by the water and the white, heat-retaining rocks. Only the wine obtained from the grapes growing on the legally designated 47.6 hectares is allowed to be called Dingač. Expect to pay around 75 kunas for a 0.7 l bottle of Dingač from the village's private winemakers, such as Ivo Skaramuča or Pavo Miličić. The Skaramuča family has been in the wine business for a long time. If you book in advance, you can try the wine produced here in the tourist info in Orebić.

## MOKALO (134 B4) (*Ⅲ J–K7*)

The INSIDER**TIP** *Adriatic campside* feels like a little garden of Eden in its location on a hillside shaded by subtropical vegetation, above the rocky coast to the east of Orebić near Mokalo. Stairs and wooden rope bridges lead down into a small, romantic bathing bay with a beach bar and to the diving school. This school also organizes trips to the 120 m (131 yd) wreck in the vicinity. There is only room for ten caravans in the upper area (it is advisable to book in advance). Camping is possible on the terraces; there are also 12 apartments in the main building, where you will also find the restaurant (*Mokalo near Orebić | tel. 020 71 34 20 | www.adriatic-mikulic.hr*).

## OREBIĆ (134 B4) (*Ⅲ J7*)

Orebić (population: 1500) stretches out for several kilometres along the island's main road and the banks of *Pelješki kanal*. The dock for the ferries to Korčula is to the west of the centre. Further in this direction you will find the recommended apartments of Villa Melita, which has pretty panoramic views, and a small pool (*9 apartments | Šet. Kneza Domagoja 47 | tel. 020 71 30 56 | www.orebic-ferien.com | Moderate*). At the pebble beach you can hire bicycles and boats and there is also a surf school (*tel. 098 39 58 07 | www. perna-surf.com*). In front of Orebić's eastern end are the beaches of Trstenica Bay. Orebić only developed in the 17th century. The people chose to live in villages away from the coasts as attacks from the sea were always possible. The town soon developed into a maritime centre. In the 19th century 33 tall ships of the local shipping company sailed the seven seas. Even though the shipping company fell victim to modern shipping, seafaring remains one of the most highly valued jobs for men in this area. Many former captains spend their retirement in houses on the sea. The ● *maritime museum* docu-

Orebić harbour on Pelješac peninsula – its history is told in the maritime museum

ments the golden age of Orebić. Since 1865 the ground floor has housed the reading room of the Pelješac captains *(summer daily 9am–noon, 5pm–8pm | 10 kunas | Trg Mimbeli)*.

The 15th century ⚜ *Franciscan priory* towers high up on the cliffs above Orebić. Among its treasures there are some valuable gifts made by the sailors *(Mon–Sat 9am–noon, 5pm–7pm, Sun 5pm–7pm | 15 kunas)*. Many captains lie buried in the cemetery next door. From up here you get wonderful panoramic views of Korčula and the offshore islands. A typical Dalmatian dish such as lamb prepared under a peka is available (after advance booking) in *Taverna Mlinica (Obala pomoraca | tel. 020 713886 | Moderate)*. Information: *Tourist Info | Zrinsko Frankopanska 2 | Orebić | tel. 020 713718 | www.tz-orebic.hr*

## STON (134 C5) (𝄢 K7)

On the seaward side of the land bridge to Pelješac peninsula, in front of the salt fields of Veliki Ston, opposite the mainland, is the smaller Mali Ston, known for its oyster and mussel farms. As a defensive measure and to protect the valuable salt flats the two neighbourhoods of Ston (population: 800) were planned and built during the Republic of Dubrovnik in the 14th century and then connected by an almost 6 km (3.7 mi) defensive wall. During the earthquake of 1996 the walls of the Romanesque and Gothic palaces in the medieval Veliki Ston cracked. Almost all of the buildings were severely damaged, some were completely destroyed. Mali Ston on the other hand remained unharmed.

The *Vila Koruna* restaurant, situated directly in front of the city walls, right on the water, serves mussel dishes and fresh oysters *(tel. 020 754359 | Moderate)*. Behind the defensive tower are two further restaurants, the *Taverna Bota* and the *Kapetanova kuća,* whose speciality is equally well-prepared seafood.

# TRIPS & TOURS

The tours are marked in green in the road atlas, in the pull-out map and on the back cover

## 1 VIS' HIDDEN TREASURES

Remote bays perfect for swimming, eccentric konoba landlords, grapevines, lavender, oleander and crystal-clear water: the island of Vis, away from the two main towns, is still a largely undiscovered beauty. The approx. 40 km (24.9 mi) island tour can be done on a scooter, or, if you are fit, by bike. You will find scooter and bike rental facilities at the harbour *(Ionios | Obala Sc. Jurija 37 | tel. 021 71 15 32)*.

The starting point is the small town of Vis → p. 76, which gave the island its name. From here the tour runs for around 10 km (6.2 mi) through the island's interior towards Komiža → p. 76 on a direct but stony route in a valley framed by mountain ranges, past the pre-Romanesque church of Sv. Mihovil, which stands on the route's highest point at 385 m (421 yd). After that there is a long, winding road down to the sea and to Komiža. Shortly before reaching the small town, your route turns off to the southwest towards Ravno, but then climbs again and goes around the island's highest mountain, Hum (587 m/642 yd). Vines frame the rugged coastline and you will constantly find new views opening up.

In Podšpilje there are signs pointing towards the nearby Titova špilja, Tito's Cave. The partisan leader and future Yugoslav president Josip Broz Tito had his military headquarters here in the last months of the Second World War, well

## Picturebook Dalmatia:
## out and about in the mountains
## and forests, on islands and lakes

hidden from the Germans. The cave is open to the public.

Before going back to the main road, why not stop by in the ● **Konoba Pol Murvu** in the village of **Žena Glava**. It is hard to believe, but the lifestyle magazine *Vanity Fair* chose this tiny remote eatery as the world's best grill *(tel. 021 715117 | Budget–Moderate)*. The grilled dishes are delicious, but so are the peka dishes, lamb and, unusually, octopus. Since there is another very original konoba along the way, leave some room for more tasty treats.

The road now runs above the coast through a *polje,* a fertile valley created by a karst depression. Once in the small town of **Plisko Polje** there are two gorgeous bays that should not be missed. You can drive all the way to Žužeca, then you have to continue on foot down the steep path to INSIDER TIP **Uvala Stiniva**, a bay that is only open to the sea through a narrow opening in the rock. It is framed by high rock walls and its water is turquoise-green thanks to the bright white of the pebbles.

The next bay along is similarly attractive. Uvala Travna requires some walking, but you will be welcomed by the extremely hospitable Senko Karuza, whose 😊 Konoba Senko is legendary. The artist, poet and chef only cooks and serves fish he caught and vegetables he grew himself. This can take hours, but it tastes delicious! The attractive pebble beach makes up for the long wait. At the end of it all the chef makes his guests wash the dishes, in the sea of course, because freshwater is a valuable commodity here *(tel. 091 33 32 99 | Budget)*.

Leaving Plisko Polje behind, stay on the main road eastbound for around 1500 m before heading southwards towards Rukavac. From this small town situated in a bay set in green, you can take a boat trip to the island of Ravnik with the lesser-known but equally attractive Zelena Špilja (Green Cave). The boats running this trip can be found in the harbour. If you still have not seen enough beautiful beaches, you could visit Uvala Srebrena, Silver Bay to the west of the town.

Once back in Plisko Polje, have someone give you directions to INSIDER TIP Stončica Bay, a further secret tip on Vis, because you will be rewarded by a sandy beach here. From the carpark above the beach there is a footpath down to the sand; food and drink are served in the simple Konoba Stončica *(tel. 021 71 16 69 | Budget)*. From Stončica it is another 4 km (2.5 mi) to the town of Vis.

Getting there takes some effort, but Uvala Stiniva is one of the most beautiful bays on Vis

## 2 FROM THE ADRIATIC TO THE LAKES IN THE HINTERLAND

Kornati, Paklenica, Plitvice Lakes, Krka – barren karst dominates the appearance of northern Dalmatia's national parks; the contrast between the karst landscape and the mellow Adriatic coast with its lavish vegetation is enormous. Organized day trips from the mainland and island holiday hotspots between Zadar and Šibenik will take you by boat to Kornati Islands National Park. From Zadar you can go on a round trip of the three remaining national parks: after the wild gorge of the Paklenica, there is the magical waterworld of the Plitvice Lakes further inland and finally, back on the coast, the spirited cascades of the Krka river. Length: approx. 350 km (217 mi) in total. Duration: at least four days, if you want to visit all four national parks. The entry fee has to be paid on the access roads.

Around 30 km (18.6 mi) from the mainland are around 148 curiously round, greyish-green, almost completely bare islands and reefs out in the sea. The ★ Kornati archipelago (Kornati Islands National Park) is a natural barrier, protecting the mainland from the waves coming in from the west from the open sea. The islands, children of the karst, are the peaks of an underwater mountain range. A few of them are inhabited, but only during the summer months. Some of the people who come here are holidaymakers who rent old fishing huts because they want to live in isolation like Robinson Crusoe.

For those with an interest in the sea, the Kornati archipelago is an extremely diverse and popular holiday destination. Marinas can be found on the islands of Piškera and Žut (Information: www.

aci-club.hr). During the summer months mariners and holidaymakers will find plenty of restaurants and taverns on the islands. There is Konoba Žakan in a bay in the south of Ravni Žakan (tel. 091 377 60 15 | Expensive) island or Konoba Ante in Vrulje Bay on the island of Kornat (tel. 022 43 50 25 | Moderate). An organized day trip including picnic costs around 300 kunas, while the entry fee to the national park depends on the size of the boat but starts at 150 kunas. Information: Kornati Islands National Park | Murter | tel. 022 43 57 40 | www.kornati.hr

Where the water does not immediately seep through the porous limestone, where boisterous rivers constantly drench the ground, you will find fresh green vegetation. This typical karst phenomenon characterizes all three national parks on the mainland: Paklenica, Krka and Plitvice Lakes.

Back in Zadar → p. 46 the tour continues northwards along the Adriatic Highway towards Rijeka and over Maslenica Bridge to Paklenica National Park. At the southern end of Croatia's largest mountain range, the Velebit, the Velika Paklenica and the Mala Paklenica gush through two magnificent, bizarre gorges. The area between the Velebit peak of Vaganski vrh (1758 m/1922 yd) and the coastal road has been declared a national park (entrance fee depending on season starting at 30 kunas). The older inhabitants of Stari Grad-Paklenica still remember the 1960s, when 'Old Surehand' rode along the rugged rock walls in front of rolling cameras and they were allowed to be part of the action as cowboys or Indians.

The modern-day heroes here are rock climbers, whose daring manoeuvres can be watched on the 400 m (437 yd) Anić kuk rock face. A hiking trail, easygoing in some places and steep in others, will take you through the gorge of **Velika Paklenica** in two hours, past several mills to the **Lugarnica** hut *(May–Oct 10.30am–4.30pm)*, where you will be able to get simple dishes and drinks *(Information: Paklenica National Park | Dr. F. Tudjmana 14 | Starigrad-Paklenica | tel. 023 36 91 55 | www.paklenica.hr)*. Various trekking tours and bird-watching hikes are available. To get to the next

A veritable miracle of nature: the Plitvice Lakes

destination of this car tour, ● ★ **Plitvice Lakes National Park**, take a left turn in front of Maslenica Bridge on to the E 71 towards Karlovac and Zagreb, a route that will lead you via **Gračac**, **Udbina** and **Korenica**. The main road crosses the dry and stony Krajina. The 200 sq km (77 sq mi) region, a national park since 1928 *(winter daily 9am–4pm, spring/autumn daily 8am–6pm, summer daily 7am–8pm | April–Oct 110 kunas, otherwise 80 kunas)*, forms a depression that is surrounded by forested mountains ranging from 500 (547) to 630 m (690 yd). Its 16 larger and smaller lakes, with their crystal-clear bluish-green water, are all in a line, connected via gushing waterfalls and foaming cascades that can be approached via wooden walkways. This enchanting landscape has been a Unesco World Heritage Site since 1979. Good accommodation is available in **Hotel Jezero** *(229 rooms | tel. 053 75 10 15 | Moderate)*. *Information: Plitvice Lakes National Park | Plitvička jezera | tel. 053 75 10 15 | www.np-plitvicka-jezera.hr*

The 111 sq km (43 sq mi) ★ **Krka National Park** *(entrances at Lozovac and Skradin daily 9am–5pm, entrance at Roški slap daily 10am–5pm | 30–100 kunas, depending on the season)* is another popular destination for visitors to Dalmatia. To get to it from Plitvice Lakes National Park, take the E 71 southbound, driving towards **Šibenik** via Gračac and Knin. The Krka carries a lot of water and is a typical karst river. From its source near Knin to where it flows into the Adriatic, it forms several eddies and waterfalls as well as many dammed lakes lined by reeds and rushes.

From **Kninsko polje** to **Skradin Bridge** the national park, which is home to 221 bird species, follows the course of the Krka. The heart of the river is the 46 m **Skradinski buk**, a unique chain of successive waterfalls, the highest tufa barrier in Europe. From here a boat departs every hour to the river island of **Visovac**, whose Franciscan priory contains a collection of valuable books and records. You can take your own boat to sail up the Krka all the way to **Skradin**. Accommodation is available in the small **Hotel Skradinski buk** *(28 rooms | tel. 022 771771 | www.skradinskibuk.hr | Budget). Information: Krka National Park | Trg Ivana Pavla II br. 5 | Šibenik | tel. 022 217720 | www.npkrka.hr*

### 3 NATURE AND TRANQUILLITY: HIKING IN MLJET NATIONAL PARK

The magical natural spectacle in the northwest of Mljet → p. 94 island can be experienced by hikers on the waymarked paths and trails that run through the national park (entry fee 100 kunas). An attractive round trip sets off from Polače on Montokuc (253 m, highest peak in the national park) and down to Veliko jezero, the island's large lake. The tour lasts approximately 3 hours for reasonably fit walkers. Good shoes are advisable, because the paths tend to be stony and damp. Do not forget to take food and a swimsuit: there are many places to stop for a picnic and enjoy a dip in the lake.

The 54 sq km (21 sq mi) **INSIDER TIP** Mljet National Park *(www.np-mljet.hr)* contains the lakes **Mali jezero** and **Veliko jezero**, which are connected to each other as well as to the sea by narrow channels. Forests of Aleppo pines, holm oaks and dense maquis grow all around them. Take the time to enjoy this forested landscape with its lakes, mountains and the sea as you hike in this park.

In order to get to the wonderful viewpoint on top of Mount Montokuc, follow the sign in **Polače → p. 95**. Walk along this path through the pine

Mljet: saltwater lakes, an island convent and nice hiking trails

forest of **Barbarioc**, created in Roman times, for about 1000 m, when you will come across a turning to **Montokuc** (approx. 45 mins). Enjoy the view of the green national park and the open sea with the islands of Korčula and Lastovo as well as Pelješac in the background. There is a small hut on top of Mount Montokuc, which is occupied by a fire watchman during the summer months. There is a sign pointing you towards the descent to **Veliko jezero → p. 95** (approx. 45 mins). Walk westwards along its shores and you will get to **Pristaniste** after about 1km. You will find a small grocery shop here, the jetty for the convent island of **Sv. Marija** and the seat of the national park administration.

Now walk along the road towards **Polače** for 500 m until you reach the large carpark. To the right of it you will find the ancient Roman trail back down to Polače.

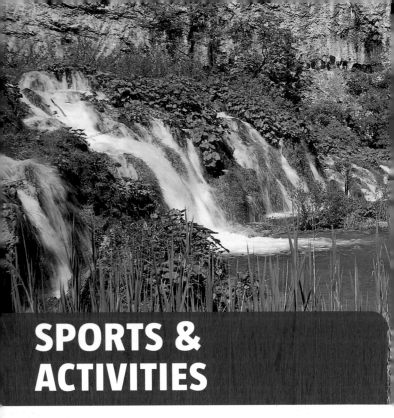

# SPORTS & ACTIVITIES

**The coast of Dalmatia is no longer all about sailing, surfing, diving and snorkelling.**

Marked hiking and mountain biking trails as well as climbing routes have opened up many new possibilities for an active getaway, particularly during the off season.

## ADVENTURE

Several Croatian travel agencies now organize tours lasting from one day to several days, on which various sporting activities can be combined. Book with Dalmatia Trekking to hike above Cetina Gorge, then climb down into the gorge the following day and end the trip with a river rafting adventure *(approx.*

*1000 kunas | Gundulićeva 22 | Split | tel. 09 58 17 3156 | www.dalmatiatrekking. com)*. Val Tours offer a seven-day canoeing, sea kayaking and rafting trip or you can hike between Krka National Park and Cetina Gorge *(approx. 5000 kunas | Trg hrvatskih velikana | biograd na moru | tel. 023 38 64 79 | www.val-tours.hr)*.

## CYCLING & MOUNTAIN BIKING

Even though the cycling network is still under construction, the islands and Dalmatia's hilly hinterland have grown into a popular destination for cycling and mountain-bike fans. Brochures with ideas for trips are available from the regional

Photo: Plitvice Lakes National Park

## ... and action!
## On foot, by mountain bike,
## by sea kayak or on a surf board

tourism boards, while all larger towns have bicycle and mountain bike rentals. Organizers will also help you go island hopping with your bike: you can make your way through the old villages and the island landscapes on a mountain bike. At the end of every route you will be welcomed by your floating means of transportation, a nostalgic motorized sailboat that will carry your bike from island to island. One such operator is 2 Wheel Treks (http://2wheeltreks.co.uk).

For descriptions of a range of tours that you can plan yourself, see *www.takead venture.com.*

### DIVING & SNORKELLING

Thanks to its many small islands and reefs and an incredibly biodiversity, the Croatian Adriatic is a paradise for divers and snorkellers. You can even see fish, crabs and octopuses when snorkelling from the beach. Almost every holiday town has diving bases and schools. Divers will need a diving licence, which is only issued by the diving schools upon presentation of diving qualifications (100 kunas for one year). *Information: Croatian Tourist Board | tel. 069 2 38 53 50 | www.croatia.hr*

## FISHING

You will need a fishing licence if you want to fish privately. This is true for inland lakes and the sea. You can get one-day fishing licences on the spot from angling shops or tourist information offices.

## FREE CLIMBING

Do you love a bit of adrenaline on a steep rock face? Close to the coast Paklenica National Park and Cetina Gorge are considered the best free-climbing areas. The climbing conditions in the 1600 m (1750 yd) karst gorges Velika and Mala Paklenica are ideal, offering 180 routes varying from difficulty 3 to 8+. The 400 m (437 yd) Anića kuk is particularly popular with rock climbers. If you plan to go climbing here, you will find lots of useful information in the multilingual climbing guide *Paklenica*, published by Boris Čujić. It is available from the national park administration *(Information: Paklenica national park administration | tel. 023 36 91 55 | www.paklenica.hr).*

On the steep cliffs of Cetina Gorge, above the small town of Omiš, around 50 free-climbing routes have been established *(Information: Tourist Info Omiš | tel. 021 86 13 50 | www.tz-omis.hr).*

## HIKING

Interesting hiking trails in an attractive landscape can be found on the islands of Brač, Hvar and Korčula, in the national

park of Mljet Island and in the northwest of the Pelješac peninsula. On the mainland the hiking trails in the national parks (Paklenica, Plitvice Lakes and Krka) and the nature parks (Velebit and Biokovo) are waymarked.

For the haute route Dalmacija, 120 km (75 mi) through central Dalmatia's mountains (Kozjak, Mosor, Biokovo), where you will find rare plants, you should plan about seven days. The paths are uniformly marked by a white dot surrounded by a red circle. Guided hiking trips lasting one or more days are organized by *Biokovo Active Holidays, Kralja Petra Kresimira | Makarska | tel. 021 67 96 55 | www.biokovo.net).*

## RAFTING, CANOEING & SEA KAYAKING

Crystal-clear mountain rivers are perfect for whitewater sports. They gush through the rocky gorges in the barren karst landscape behind the coast. In northern Dalmatia tours are run on the Krupa and the

Zlatni rat near Bol on the island of Brač is considered one of Dalmatia's top surfing spots

Zrmanja, by, for example, *Val Tours (tel. 023 38 64 79 | www.val-tours.hr)*, while Cetina Gorge is a good location in central Dalmatia *(Information: rafting association in Omiš | tel. 021 86 31 61 | www.raft. hr)*.

One activity that is popular right now is a relaxed paddle on the sea. ☺ *Sea kayaking* combines the sporting aspect with the opportunity of getting in an environmentally friendly manner to bays that are only accessible from the water. Almost every larger seaside town has a kayak rental facility *(price for a single kayak is around 7 kunas per hour)*. The Elaphiti Islands near Dubrovnik are particularly suitable and popular for extended kayaking tours *(www.adriaadventure.hr)*.

## WINDSURFING, SAILING & KITE SURFING

Windsurfing is possible almost everywhere. Surfing equipment and courses are offered in most holiday resorts. Because of the strong mistral winds in the afternoons, the Pelješki kanal between Korčula and Pelješac as well as Zlatni rat near Bol on the island of Brač are considered the best spots for the more experienced. Rentals and courses offered by *Big Blue Sport (Bol | tel. 021 63 56 14 | www.big-blue-sport.hr)*.

The 56 marinas along the Croatian mainland coast and on the islands have a mooring capacity of more than 16,000. The shipping stronghold is northern Dalmatia because of the Kornati archipelago. Information from the *Croatian Tourist Board (tel. 069 2 38 53 50 | www. croatia.hr has a list of sailing clubs and links to their websites)* or from *ACI (Adriatic Croatia International Club | M. Tita 151 | Opatija | tel. 051 27 12 88 | www.aci-club.hr)*. Up-to-date information and tips are exchanged by insiders on *www. skippertipps.de*.

Kite surfing has been growing in popularity for quite a few years now. Beginners will need calm waters, which can be found around Nin as well as near Bol on the island of Brač.

# TRAVEL WITH KIDS

Most pebble and rock beaches on the Dalmatian coast are framed by vegetation that provides welcome shade. The best shallow pebble beaches can be found along the Makarska Riviera.

Nature only blessed Dalmatia with a few modest sandy beaches. They can be found in Lumbarda on Korčula, in Saharun Bay on Dugi otok and around the lagoon in front of the small town of Nin. Little ones will be able to splash about without danger in the children's pools of the holiday resorts.

Like everywhere in the south, it is customary to take children to restaurants, museums, exhibitions and festivals, even late at night. Enjoy the mellow summer nights with your children and put them down for a Dalmatian *pižolot* (nap) in the heat of day.

## ZADAR REGION

### ADVENTURE PARK
(130 C4) (*Ⅲ E3*)

In Kožino, just a few kilometres from Zadar, there is a challenging high-ropes park in a spruce forest. After a brief instruction, the children (and adults) practise their skills on swaying planks, lurching rope ladders and various other hair-raising obstacles – all well-secured of course. *Summer daily 9am until sunset | entrance fee 90 kunas | Kožino*

### INSIDER TIP ► KALPIĆ FAMILY FARM
(132 B2) (*Ⅲ G4*)

The Kalpić family personally take young and old visitors around their farm in

Photo: Exploring the Kornati archipelago by boat

Acrobats and pirates – Croats love children and have lots of fun to offer them

the hinterland of Šibenik, showing them the vineyard and the fig trees, from which you are allowed to pick a fruit or two. The large neighbouring field is a great place to romp around. To make sure you keep your strength up you will be served home-made ham and sheep's cheese with freshly baked flatbread and home-pressed wine. *17 km (10.6 mi) northeast of Šibenik, away from the road to Knin in the village of Radonić | tel. 091 584 55 20 | www.agrotour-kalpic.com*

### FALCONRY
(132 B2) (*ω G4*)

Face to face with falcons, buzzards and hawks: 18 birds of prey are in the constant care of Emilio Mendjušić in Croatia's only falconry centre, which is primarily dedicated to the care of injured raptors, after which they are reintroduced into the wild. Emilio demonstrates his daily work to visitors, such as feeding the birds as they sit on a thick glove on his hand. Even under guidance it is an exciting feeling to INSIDER TIP hold out the prey for a swooping buzzard. The *Sokolarski Centar* is situated on the edge of the village of Dubrava. *Mon–Sat 10am–7pm | 20 kunass | 8 km (5 mi) southeast of Šibenik, leave Šibenik to the northeast on the Kralja Zvonimira, turn right after 5 km (3.1 mi) on to the 6091*

## BEAR CUBS
(130 C1) (*∅ E1*)

The village of Kuterevo in the Velebit mountains, around 30 km (18.6 mi) from the coast and from Senj, is home to bears! An animal welfare initiative has set up an enclosure for brown bears who have lost their mothers and would not be able to survive on their own in the wilderness. Lost, injured and sick young bears from all over Croatia are brought to Kuterevo. The goal is to reintroduce the bears back into the wild once they are old enough. Until then they are kept well in large enclosures where visitors can watch them as they play around, play-fight or nap. The littlest ones are particularly cute. *May–Nov sunrise to sunset | entrance fee 22 kunas | Velebitsko utočište za mlade medvjede Kuterevo | Pod crikvom 103 | Kuterevo | tel. 053 79 92 22*

Every child will love splashing in the water on Croatia's gently shelving beaches

# SPLIT REGION

## BATHING ON A FAMILY-FRIENDLY BEACH (133 D4) (*∅ J5*)

The pebble beach of *Punta Rata* in *Brela* is considered one of the most family-friendly in the whole of Croatia. It shelves so gently that even very small children can splash around safely in the water. The pebbles are small and a lot more pleasant than the sharp stones of the rocky beaches. A small pine forest provides shade and there are several cafés serving child-friendly snacks.

## BATHING IN THE CITY
(132 C3) (*∅ H5*)

Children cannot be interested for too long in the churches, palaces and museums in the old town of Split. When even the promise of ice creams is no longer adequate compensation for boredom, take a break on a beach or in a forest. It is around a 20-minute walk from Diocletian's palace to the city beach of *Bačvice*, a respectable leisure centre in a shallow pebbly bay behind the ferry quays. On the west side of the old town is the forested park of Marjan, criss-crossed by many trails. There is also a playground near *Varoš* viewpoint.

### PLAYING CAPTAIN

Drifting along on one of the replica historical sailboats through Croatia's islands, helping to hoist the anchor, bathing in remote bays, throwing out the anchor in front of 'pirate nests' and jumping into crystal-clear waters straight from the boat: all of these things are fun for children. The fact that they will walk along fortress walls, stroll around historic towns and splash about in the water on family-friendly beaches just adds to their enjoyment. Local tourist information offices will provide information about day and mini cruises.

### WHAT'S GROWING?
(133 E4) (*ØØ J6*)

Hundreds of native plant species flourish on the edge of Biokovo Nature Park in the 16.5 hectare *Kotišina Botanical Gardens*; stone plaques bear the names of the individual species. *Free entry | Kotišina 3 km (1.9 mi) north of Makarska*

## DUBROVNIK REGION

### ISLAND HOPPING FROM GRUŽ ●
(129 D5) (*ØØ L7*)

Have your little ones had enough of beach shoes and stony beaches? Then take a boat trip to the island of *Lopud*. The journey there from Dubrovnik's harbour, Gruž, on the old ferry is an adventure. In addition to the passengers, all kinds of goods and food are carried across to supply the inhabitants of the Elaphiti Islands. Go for a short walk in Lopud through the wild maquis to reach the beach, where you will finally be able to build some sandcastles. If you like, you can take the ferry further to Koločep and Šipan. But make sure not to miss the last boat back. The timetable is available at *www.jadrolinija.hr*

An adventure with a view – exploring the country

### DIVING FOR CHILDREN
(133 D5) (*ØØ H7*)

Children only have to be eight years old to be welcome in the kids' programme of the *Croatia Divers* diving school. Bobby and Marjolein will take eight to ten-year-olds on the two-hour *PADI Bubblemaker* taster session, during which the children will dive with a mask and a bottle for 30 minutes *(around 350 kunas)*. Children of ten and over can also participate in the junior programme, which will allow them to obtain the *Padi junior Open Water Diver* certificate. *Obala 1 | Vela Luka | Korčula | tel. 020 813508 | www.croatiadivers.com*

# FESTIVALS & EVENTS

If you cannot sing and do not like wine, then you are not a real Dalmatian, according to the Dalmatians themselves, and they prove as much all year round. The programme ranges from religious festivals such as the Good Friday procession to the children's festival. A klapa (a group of friends) does not need anything but the pure joy of singing in order to spontaneously sing the jolly to melancholy melodies that capture the Dalmatian attitude. These singers appear in traditional costumes at festivals and events.

## OFFICIAL HOLIDAYS

**1 Jan** *New Year's Day,* **6 Jan** *Epiphany,* **March/April** *Easter,* **1 May** *Labour Day,* **22 June** *Anti-Fascist Struggle Day,* **25 June** *Statehood Day,* **5 Aug** *Victory Day,* **15 Aug** *Assumption,* **8 Oct** *Independence Day,* **1 Nov** *All Saints,* **25/26 Dec** *Christmas*

## EVENTS & FESTIVALS

### MARCH/APRIL

▶ *Korčula:* Lively Christian custom during Holy Week, with ceremonial services and processions by the traditional All Saints' Brotherhood, the Brotherhood of St Michael and the Brotherhood of St Roch. Palm Sunday–Easter Monday

▶ *Hvar:* In the night from Maundy Thursday to Good Friday, the Cross Procession follows a 500-year-old custom, making its way through six island communities until 6am.

### MAY

▶ *Skradin: Eco-Ethno Fair* in Skradin's old town. Traditional artisans present their skills and products, while organic farmers display their fruit and vegetables. 1/2 May

### JUNE

▶ *Šibenik: International Children's Festival*, during which the entire town is transformed into a large stage for music, theatre, acrobatics and colourful games. From mid-June for two weeks

### JULY/AUGUST

▶ *Korčula: Moreška –* this festival, which takes place at the beginning of July and involves chivalrous jousting and sword dancing in colourful, medieval costumes, reminds Korčula's inhabitants of their struggle against the Turks.

▶ *Omiš: Klapa Festival –* klapa groups

## Church processions, classical music concerts or events on horseback: the people of Dalmatia are always in the mood to celebrate

from all over Dalmatia meet in July to engage in a jolly singing contest.

▶ *Dubrovnik:* ★ *Summer Festival* – large music and theatre festival on 33 open air stages in the old town. The programme ranges from classical, jazz, folk and theatre to art exhibitions. Mid-July–end of August.

▶ *Split: Splitsko ljeto* (Split Summer) – drama, ballet and opera festival on open-air stages in the old town. Firm fixtures include performances of Verdi's *Aida* and *Nabucco* in the peristyle. Mid-July–mid-August

▶ *Zadar: Music Festival in Sv. Donat* – religious music from the Middle Ages, the Renaissance and the Baroque. July–mid-August

▶ *Dugi otok: Saljske Užance* – in Sali the donkeys are let loose to race. Wine, food and music accompany this event. 1st week in August

▶ *Kukljica, Ugljan: Madona od snijega* (Our Lady of the Snows) – ceremonial procession of boats. 5 Aug.

▶ *Sinj:* ★ *Sinjska alka* – Croatia's most significant folkloristic festival of chivalry. The participants dress up in magnificent uniforms. The event has been held since 1715 to commemorate the Croatian victory over the Turks. The event is held on the same days as the religious festival of the Madonna of Sinj, to whom, according to legend, the *alkari* (riders) owe their victory. A three-day festival on the 1st weekend in August *(www.alka.hr)*

### SEPTEMBER

▶ *Korčula: Marco Polo Days* – the highlight is the re-enactment of the historic battle of Korčula 1298, during which Marco Polo, allegedly born in Korčula, was taken captive. 1st or 2nd week in September

▶ INSIDER TIP *Murter: Latinsko idro* – with a week focusing on the 'Latin' sail, Murter brings the traditional Adriatic boats back to life; the highlight is the Michaelmas regatta at the end of September.

# NOTES

# LINKS, BLOGS, APPS & MORE

LINKS

▶ www.undp.hr/show.jsp?page=80240 The UN's English-language website provides information about development and environmental programmes being carried out along the Croatian coast with UN support

▶ www.inyourpocket.com/croatia Dalmatia is represented on this English homepage with the City Guides Dubrovnik, Split and Zadar. Topical tips on shopping, eating, drinking and nightlife are rounded off with users' comments

▶ www.croatia-beaches.com Looking for the most beautiful, most romantic, most family-friendly or sandiest beach? This website will allow you to search by all conceivable criteria and lead you in the end to your dream beach

BLOGS & FORUMS

▶ www.find-croatia.com/blog/ Blog with photos and videos of Croatia

▶ www.croatia-blog.net/en/ Blogs and podcasts on everything to do with travelling in Croatia - reports, practical tips, and forums dealing with politics, business and sport

▶ http://croatiatraveller.com/blog/ Numerous contributions subdivided into categories such as Accommodation, Travel, Adventure...

▶ secretdalmatia.wordpress.com Interesting blogs on Dalmatia's gastronomy, culture and sights, with good photos and links

▶ www.expat-blog.com/en/directory/europe/croatia/ Would you like to work, live, move to Croatia? Or just to find out how is life in Croatia? Expats report on their experiences

Regardless of whether you are still preparing your trip or already in Dalmatia: these addresses will provide you with more information, videos and networks to make your holiday even more enjoyable.

▶ www.crovideos.com From the simple holiday movie to informative documentaries on customs and music – this site is also home to numerous videos about Dalmatia. There are also Croatian hits in MP3 format to download

▶ www.about-croatia.com/croatian-videos/ Wide collection of videos on Croatia broken down by category (coast, islands, interior...)

▶ www.travelpod.com/travel-blog-country/Croatia/tpod.html Good photos along with numerous videos and blogs in English

▶ http://galijula.izor.hr/web/guest/pokretne-slike-s-kamere Is the sun shining on Split? Are there boats at anchor? The live webcam of the Oceanographic Institute will tell you

▶ HotelRadar Are you looking for the neaqrest hotels in Dubrovnik or Zadar? No problem with this little app, assessment and booking included

▶ Croatia Traffic & Weather Weather, tail-backs, radar traps, ferry connections and regatta schedules – this English-language app has everything for your Croatian trip

▶ ProGuides–Croatia Travel guide for the major cities, from Zagreb via Split to Dubrovnik

▶ www.seekcroatia.com This social network site in English deals with travelling in Croatia

▶ www.virtualtourist.com/travel/Europe/Croatia/TravelGuide-Croatia.html The Croats are very active on this network, and contribute numerous comments and tips from their home towns

▶ http://hr-hr.facebook.com/croatia.hr?sk=app_10467688569 Croatia on Facebook, with tips from sightseeing to activities, lots of photos

# TRAVEL TIPS

## ARRIVAL

There is no continuous motorway connection to southern Dalmatia. The fastest eastern route runs via Ljubljana and Novo Mesto / Slovenia to Karlovac / Croatia and via Zadar to Split. The western route goes through Trieste / Italy, Koper / Slovenia and Rijeka to the coast. Rapid progress is being made in Croatia on extending the motorway to Dubrovnik (information about the current situation: *www.hac.hr*). Slovenian and Croatian motorways are toll roads.

EuroCity trains to Zagreb depart from Germany and Austria. Some trains have through coaches to Rijeka, national trains also to Zadar, Šibenik and Split.

There are coaches to Zagreb, Rijeka and Split departing from many major towns. From there you can find connections to Croatia's very well developed public bus network.

Scheduled flights with, for example, Croatia Airlines *(www.croatiaair lines.hr)* flies direct to and from Dubrovnik and Split from London Heathrow and Gatwick. A number of Europe's discount carriers serve Croatia, e.g. Ryanair flies to Rijeka from London Stansted and to Zadar from Stansted and Dublin, Easyjet to Dubrovnik from Stansted and Dublin.

An attractive alternative to taking the motorway and the coastal road is taking the car ferry southwards past the big and small islands along the Dalmatian coast (duration: approx. 24 hrs.). The ferries depart from Rijeka and go via Split, Stari Grad (Hvar), Korčula and Sobra (Mljet) all the way to Dubrovnik. There are also car ferries from Ancona to Zadar and from Bari to Dubrovnik. Ferry prices: 4-berth cabin starting at 400 kunas per person, without a cabin from 210 kunas, vehicles from 580 kunas. Information at *www.jadrolinija.hr*

## RESPONSIBLE TRAVEL

It doesn't take a lot to be environmentally friendly whilst travelling. Don't just think about your carbon footprint whilst flying to and from your holiday destination but also about how you can protect nature and culture abroad. As a tourist it is especially important to respect nature, look out for local products, cycle instead of driving, save water and much more. If you would like to find out more about eco-tourism please visit: *www.ecotourism.org*

## BANKS

Banks are usually open *Mon–Fri 7am–7pm, Sat 7am–1pm*. You will find ATMs in the tourist towns, where you can take money out with debit and credit cards.

## BUSES

One alternative for excursions without parking problems is to use the good bus network, which also covers smaller towns along the coast and on the islands.

Buses are frequent, regular and inexpensive. The journey from Split to Dubrovnik costs 150 kunas for example.

## CAMPING

Camping and caravanning are not allowed outside of designated sites. Most of Croatia's campsites – there are more than 520 – are on the Adriatic coast. Croatia has modernized most of its sites to conform to enhanced international standards.

Most of the campsites attract guests with many extras such as mini clubs, aqua parks, a wide array of sporting activities and restaurants as well as nightclubs and perfect holiday villages. In some places you can also rent apartments and bungalows. If large sites with more than a thousand pitches are not your thing, you will also find smaller ones. Naturists will appreciate the high standards in the naturist camps. A list and descriptions of the campsites can be found at *www.camping.hr.*

## CAR HIRE

Car rental places can be found in every sizeable holiday resort. The requirements for renting a vehicle are not the same everywhere. In most cases you need to be at least 21 and have had two years' driving experience. A medium-sized vehicle will cost around 300 kunas a day.

## CUSTOMS

You are allowed to import your personal provisions without incurring customs charges. You may also import 500 g of coffee, 200 cigarettes, 1 l of spirits, 2 l of wine, 50 ml of perfume or 25 ml of Eau de toilette and other goods up to a value of 300 kunas.

The same quantities apply when re-entering the EU. All valuables other than standard luggage items (including cameras and laptops), as well as cash worth more than 10,000 kunas should be declared.

## CURRENCY CONVERTER

| £ | HRK | HRK | £ |
|---|---|---|---|
| 1 | 8.45 | 1 | 0.12 |
| 3 | 25 | 3 | 0.35 |
| 5 | 42 | 5 | 0.59 |
| 13 | 110 | 13 | 1.54 |
| 40 | 338 | 40 | 4.73 |
| 75 | 634 | 75 | 8.88 |
| 120 | 1,013 | 120 | 14.20 |
| 250 | 2,112 | 250 | 29.60 |
| 500 | 4,225 | 500 | 59.20 |

| $ | HRK | HRK | $ |
|---|---|---|---|
| 1 | 5.15 | 1 | 0.19 |
| 3 | 15.50 | 3 | 0.58 |
| 5 | 26 | 5 | 0.97 |
| 13 | 67 | 13 | 2.52 |
| 40 | 206 | 40 | 7.75 |
| 75 | 387 | 75 | 14.53 |
| 120 | 620 | 120 | 23.25 |
| 250 | 1,290 | 250 | 48.45 |
| 500 | 2,580 | 500 | 97.00 |

For current exchange rates see www.xe.com

# BUDGETING

| | | |
|---|---|---|
| Coffee | 9 kunas | in a café bar for one espresso |
| Ice cream | 9 kunas | for two scoops |
| Snacks | 36–60 kunas | for a pizza |
| Museum | 15–22 kunas | per person |
| Fuel | 7.85 kunas | for 1 l of petrol (95 ROZ) |
| Deck chair | 35–60 kunas | per day |

## DRINKING WATER

Tap water is drinkable almost everywhere, but it is often heavily chlorinated. Since the mineral water in PET bottles is tastier and also inexpensive, it is better to choose that option instead.

## DRIVING

National registration and a national driving licence are enough. The green insurance card is required for all vehicles. If you are not coming to Croatia with your own vehicle, you will need to be authorized by the owner.

Speed limits: 50 km/h (30 mph) in towns, 90 km/h (55 mph) outside towns, 110 km/h (70 mph) on expressways and 130 km/h (80 mph) on motorways. Towing vehicles outside towns 80 km/h (50 mph). The legal alcohol limit is 50 mg per 100 ml.

During the winter months you must switch on your headlights (dipped) during the day too. School buses must not be overtaken when children are getting in and out. Any crash (a high-visibility jacket is mandatory) has to be reported to the police, who will issue confirmation of the damage; this will avoid potential problems on leaving Croatia.

Croatia has a well-developed network of service stations and petrol stations; all types of fuel are available in sufficient quantity at EU quality. Croatian motorways are toll roads. The Croatian breakdown service HAK is staffed around the clock: *tel. 987.*

## EMBASSIES

**US EMBASSY**
*Andrije Hebranga 2 | Zagreb | Tel. 01 6 61 22 00 | http://zagreb.usembassy.gov*

**UK EMBASSY**
*Vlaska 121 | Zagreb | Tel. 01 4 55 53 10 | http://ukincroatia.fco.gov.uk/en/*

**IRISH CONSULATE**
*Turinina ulica 3 | Zagreb | Tel. 01 667 44 55 | acsain@cpad.hr*

**CANADIAN EMBASSY**
*Prilaz Gjure Dezelica 4 | Zagreb | Tel. 01 488 1200 | http://croatia.gc.ca*

**AUSTRALIAN EMBASSY**
*Centar Kaptol, 3rd floor Nova Ves 11 | Zagreb | Tel. 01 4891 200 | http://www.croatia.embassy.gov.au*

**NZ CONSULATE**
*Hrvatska matica iseljenika, Trg Stjepana Radica 3 | Zagreb | Tel. 01 6151 382 | nzea landconsulate@matis.hr*

## EMERGENCY NUMBERS

Police *(policija)*: tel. 192;
Fire brigade *(vatrogasci)*: tel. 93;
Rescue *(hitna pomoć)*: tel. 94

## IMMIGRATION

For a maximum stay of 90 days EU (and US) citizens will need an ID card or passport that is valid for the duration of their stay. The same is true for people who travel through Bosnia Herzegovina near Neum on the coastal road to southern Dalmatia.

## FERRIES

The regional ferry connections to the islands, the coastal route from Rijeka to Dubrovnik, as well as the internationally ferry services to Italy and Greece are largely operated by the vessels of the national shipping company *Jadrolinija*. It is not possible to reserve seats on regional services. For that reason drivers should queue up well before the ship's departure. Embarkation begins 2–3 hours before the scheduled sailing time, while it begins immediately upon arrival at the ports en route. Passengers with reservations have to report to the harbour office at least two hours before the ship leaves *(www.jadrolinija.hr)*.

## HEALTH

There are no special health risks in Dalmatia. It is important to take good precautions against the sun. Bring a cooling gel to treat sunburns and mosquito bites as well as beach shoes to provide protection against sharp rocks and sea urchins. Hikers visiting the islands should take proper boots that have a good ankle support. A higher boot is also advisable because of the many snakes, some of which are venomous.

On the mainland and the larger islands there are pharmacies as well as doctors who speak English. Addresses are available from your accommodation, the local offices of your tour operator and from the tourist information offices.

It is advisable to take out private travel insurance, to include emergency repatriation.

## INFORMATION AT YOUR DESTINATION

National information offices can be found in every major town. They are usually called *Tourist Info* or *Turistička zajednica*, abbreviated to *tz*. You will get leaflets, bus and ferry timetables and maps here. In most cases you will also be able to change money. During the peak season the offices are opened daily without a lunch break, while during the low season they are often only open in the morning or they have a longer lunch break. In addition to the national offices, there is a large number of private travel agencies often calling themselves *Tourist-Biro* or something similar; they are specialized in selling private rooms and apartments as well as excursions.

The addresses and websites of all of the tourism offices can be found at *www.croatia.hr* under the relevant destinations.

## INFORMATION BEFORE YOUR DEPARTURE

**CROATIAN NATIONAL TOURIST OFFICE**
– *Lanchesters 162–164 Fulham Palace Road, 2 | W6 9ER London | Tel. +44 208 563 7979 | info@croatia-london.co.uk*
– *350 Fifth Avenue, Suite 4003 | 10118 New York | Tel. +1 212 279 8672 | cntony@earthlink.net*
– *www.croatia.hr*
– *www.findcroatia.com*

## MONEY & PRICES

Croatia's currency is the kuna. One kuna equals a hundred lipas. Relative to Croatian wages prices are quite high. That is why many locals cannot afford to eat in a good restaurant. Groceries are also quite expensive. As a result, Croatia is no longer a cheap destination for holidaymakers as it used to be when it was still part of Yugoslavia. However, in comparison to other southern European countries you still get good value for money.

## OPENING TIMES

Most restaurants are open continuously from noon until the evening during the main season from April/May to the end of September. During the low season only some of the hotels, restaurants and shops are open in the holiday resorts. The same is true for museums, whose opening times often change even during a season. It is best to enquire on the spot in the relevant tourist information office.

## PHONES & MOBILE PHONES

It is cheapest to use a phone card and make calls from one of the many pay-phones. The instructions will appear on the display, in English, at the push of a button. The cheapest rates are available

# WEATHER IN SPLIT

| | Jan | Feb | March | April | May | June | July | Aug | Sept | Oct | Nov | Dec |
|---|---|---|---|---|---|---|---|---|---|---|---|---|
| Daytime temperatures in °C/°F | 10/50 | 11/52 | 14/57 | 18/64 | 22/72 | 27/81 | 31/88 | 31/88 | 26/79 | 21/70 | 16/61 | 11/52 |
| Nighttime temperatures in °C/°F | 5/41 | 5/41 | 7/45 | 10/50 | 14/57 | 18/64 | 21/70 | 20/68 | 17/63 | 14/57 | 11/52 | 6/43 |
| Sunshine hours/day | 4 | 5 | 6 | 7 | 9 | 10 | 12 | 11 | 8 | 6 | 4 | 3 |
| Precipitation days/month | 9 | 8 | 8 | 7 | 7 | 6 | 4 | 3 | 6 | 8 | 11 | 12 |
| Water temperature in °C/°F | 13/55 | 12/54 | 13/55 | 14/57 | 17/63 | 21/70 | 23/73 | 24/75 | 22/72 | 19/66 | 16/61 | 14/57 |

during the week after 10pm and during the day on Sundays.

The international dialling code for Croatia is 00385; Britain: 0044; North America: 001.

If you plan to use your mobile phone a lot, it will be worth your while getting a Croatian pre-paid card, such as from the Croatian T-Mobile *(www.t-mobile. hr)*. The benefit of such a card is that you will not have to pay to receive calls. Other pre-paid cards are more expensive, but you would also avoid all roaming charges. And you will get your new number before you leave home. Your mailbox could cost you a lot of money, so best switch that off before going on your trip!

## POST

The opening times of the post offices *(pošta)* are not the same everywhere, but they are usually open *Mon–Fri 7am–7pm, Sat 8am–1pm*. The cost of sending a postcard to another country is 3.50 kunas.

## SMOKING

Smoking is not allowed in any public building, restaurant or hotel in Dalmatia. Anyone disregarding this can expect to pay stiff fines.

## TIPS

Good service in a restaurant should be rewarded with around 10 percent of the bill. The time-tested rule for hotels is to sweeten the employees' job a little with an appropriate tip shortly after you arrive (from approx. 19 kunas per week) as you will benefit by receiving their attention during your stay.

## WHEN TO GO

The peak season with the highest prices in the hotels and restaurants lasts from July to August. During this time it is highly advisable to book your accommodation in advance, since all the hotels will be almost completely booked out. In addition prices are often inflated for individual travellers. It is safer and often significantly cheaper to book the same thing (possibly on a day-by-day basis) in advance through a travel agent. The first two weeks of August are particularly busy because many Italians traditionally spend their holiday in Dalmatia until *Ferragosto* (15 Aug).

The region's mild climate is characterized by Mediterranean influences. The summers tend to be sunny and warm during the day, while the nights are refreshingly cooler. From time to time black clouds build up that turn into thundershowers in the afternoon. Since the Adriatic is not particularly deep, the sea quickly warms up to 20°C / 68°F in the early summer, while temperatures of 26°C / 79°F and higher are measured in August.

The best time to go is mid-May to the end of June, when the gorse is flowering, and September, when the summer heat is not so intense anymore but the Adriatic is still pleasantly warm. During the late summer and autumn months, the cold katabatic bora wind can bring changes in the weather and choppy seas.

## WIFI

WiFi access is available now in the public spaces of most larger towns, often at the main square, and, in Dubrovnik, even in the entire old town (marked as a WiFi zone). In addition most of the *ACI (www. aci-club.hr)* marinas, almost all better business hotels and all-inclusive hotels have WiFi access.

# USEFUL PHRASES CROATIAN

## PRONUNCIATION

Here are some hints on how to pronounce Croatian:

| | |
|---|---|
| č | 'ch' as in 'church' |
| š | 'sh' as in 'shop' |
| ć | something between 'ch' and 'tya' |
| ž | like the 's' in 'pleasure' |

All vowels are open and should always be pronounced clearly. In combinations of vowels, each vowel is pronounced separately: reuma = re-oo-ma.
When 'r' forms a syllable, it must also be pronounced clearly: vrba, Krk.

In words of two syllables, the first syllable is stressed. In words of several syllables, we have marked the syllable that is stressed with a dot.

Abbreviations: coll. = colloquial; f = female speaker

### IN BRIEF

| | |
|---|---|
| Yes/No/Maybe | Da/Ne/Možda |
| Please/Thank you | Molim/Hvala |
| Excuse me, please | Oprostite molim/Oprostite molim vas |
| May I ...?/Pardon? | Smijem li ...?/Molim? |
| I would like to .../Have you got ...? | Htio ( Htjela f) bih .../Imate li ...? |
| How much is ... | Koliko košta ...? |
| I (don't) like that/good/bad | To mi se (ne) dopada/dobro/loše |
| broken/doesn't work | pokvaren/ne funkcionira |
| too much/much/little/all/nothing | previše/puno/malo/sve/ništa |
| Help!/Attention!/Caution! | Pomoć!/Upozorenje!/Oprez! |
| ambulance/police/fire brigade | vozilo za hitnu pomoć/policija/vatrogasci |
| Prohibition/forbidden/ danger/dangerous | zabrana/zabranjeno/ opasnost/opasno |

### GREETINGS, FAREWELL

| | |
|---|---|
| Good morning!/afternoon! | Dobro jutro/dobar dan! |
| Good evening!/night! | Dobar večer/laku noć |
| Hello!/Goodbye!/See you | Zdravo! (halo, bok)/Do vidjenja/Bok! (Čao!) |
| My name is ... | Moje ime je... |

# Govoriš li hrvatski?

'Do you speak Croatian?' This guide will help you to say the basic words and phrases in Croatian.

| | |
|---|---|
| What's your name? | Kako se vi zovete? (Kako Vam je ime?) |
| | Kako se ti zoveš? |
| I'm from ... | Dolazim iz ... |

## DATE & TIME

| | |
|---|---|
| Monday/Tuesday/Wednesday | ponedjeljak/utorak/srijeda |
| Thursday/Friday/Saturday | četvrtak/petak/subota |
| working day/Sunday/holiday | radni dan/nedjelja/praznik |
| today/tomorrow/yesterday | danas/sutra/jučer |
| hour/minute | sat/minuta |
| day/night/week/month/year | dan/noć/tjedan/mjesec/godina |
| What time is it? | Koliko je sati? |
| It's three o'clock/It's half past three | Sad je tri sata/Sad je pola četiri |

## TRAVEL

| | |
|---|---|
| open/closed | otvoreno/zatvoreno |
| entrance/vehicle entrance/ | ulaz/prolaz/ |
| exit/vehicle exit | izlaz/prolaz |
| departure/departure (plane)/arrival | odlazak/odletište/doletište |
| toilets/ladies/gentlemen | toalet/ženski/muški |
| (no) drinking water | (ne) pitka voda |
| Where is ...?/Where are ...? | Gdje je ...?/Gdje su ...? |
| left/right/straight ahead/back | ljevo/desno/ravno/natrag |
| close/far | blizu/daleko |
| bus/tram/taxi/stop | autobus/tramvaj/taxi (taksi)/stajalište |
| parking lot/parking garage | parkiralište/podzemna garaža |
| street map/map | plan grada/zemljopisna karta |
| train station/harbour/airport | željeznička stanica/luka/zračna luka |
| schedule/ticket/supplement | plan vožnje/vozna karta/doplatak |
| single/return | jednosmjerno/tamo i natrag |
| train/track/platform | vlak/peron/željeznički peron |
| I would like to rent ... | Želim unajmiti ... |
| a car/a bicycle/a boat | jedan auto/jedan bicikl/jedan brodić |
| petrol/gas station / petrol (gas)/diesel | pumpna stanica / benzin/dizel |
| breakdown/repair shop | nezgoda/radionica |

## FOOD & DRINK

| | |
|---|---|
| Could you please book a table for tonight for four? | Molim rezervirajte nam za večeras jedan stol za četiri osobe. |

| | |
|---|---|
| on the terrace/by the window | na terasi/uz prozor |
| The menu, please | Molim donesite jelovnik. |
| Could I please have ...? | Mogul i dobiti...? |
| bottle/carafe/glass | flašu/karafu/čašu |
| knife/fork/spoon | nož/vilicu/žlicu |
| salt/pepper/sugar/vinegar/oil | sol/papar/šećer/ocat/ulje |
| milk/cream/lemon | mljeko/vrhnje/citronu |
| cold/too salty/not cooked | hladno/presoljeno/nedopečeno |
| with/without ice/sparkling | sa/bez mjehurića (plina) |
| vegetarian/allergy | vegetarijanac(ci)/alergičar(i) |
| May I have the bill, please? | Želim platiti, molim |
| bill/tip | račun/napojnica |

## SHOPPING

| | |
|---|---|
| Where can I find...? | Gdje mogu naći ...? |
| I'd like .../I'm looking for ... | Želim .../Tražim ... |
| Do you put photos onto CD? | Možete li spržiti fotografije na CD? |
| pharmacy/chemist/baker/market | apoteka/drogerija/pekarnica/plac |
| shopping centre/department store | kupovni centar/robna kuća |
| food shop/supermarket | trgovina sa namirnicama/supermarket |
| photographic items/ | fotoartikli/ |
| newspaper shop/kiosk | novinarnica/kiosk |
| 100 grammes/1 kilo | sto grama/jedan kilo |
| expensive/cheap/price/more/less | skupo/jeftino/cijena/manje/više |
| organically grown | sa biloškog polja |

## ACCOMMODATION

| | |
|---|---|
| I have booked a room | Imam jednu sobu rezerviranu. (Rezervirao (rezervirala) sam sobu) |
| Do you have any ... left? | Imate li još ... |
| single room/double room | jednokrevetnu sobu/dvokrevetnu sobu |
| breakfast/half board/full board (American plan) | doručak/polupansion/ puni pansion |
| at the front/seafront/lakefront | prema naprijed/prema moru/prema jezeru |
| shower/sit-down bath/balcony/terrace | tuš/kadu/balkon/terasu |
| key/room card | ključ/karticu za sobu |
| luggage/suitcase/bag | prtljagu/kofer/tašnu |

## BANKS, MONEY & CREDIT CARDS

| | |
|---|---|
| bank/ATM/pin code | banka/bankomat/broj pina |
| I'd like to change ... | Želim promijeniti ... |
| cash/credit card | gotovina/ec kartica/kreditna kartica |
| bill/coin/change | papirni novac/kovanice/povratni novac |

# USEFUL PHRASES

## HEALTH

| | |
|---|---|
| doctor/dentist/paediatrician | ljecnik/zubar/djecji ljecnik |
| hospital/emergency clinic | bolnica/hitna služba |
| fever/pain/inflamed/injured | temperatura/bolovi/upala/povreda |
| diarrhoea/nausea/sunburn | proljev/povracanje/suncane opekotine |
| plaster/bandage/ointment/cream | flaster/zavoj/mast/krema |
| pain reliever/tablet/suppository | sredstvo protiv bolova/tablete/cepic |

## POST, TELECOMMUNICATIONS & MEDIA

| | |
|---|---|
| stamp | marka za pismo |
| I'm looking for a prepaid card for my mobile | Trebam pokretnu/prepaid karticu za moj mobilni telefon |
| Where can I find internet access? | Gdje mogu naci internet kafe? |
| Do I need a special area code? | Trebam li posebni pozivni broj? |
| dial/connection/engaged | birati/spojeno/zauzeto |
| socket/adapter/charger | uticnica/adapter-prilagodac/punjac |
| computer/battery/rechargeable battery | kompjuter/baterija/akumulator |
| internet address (URL)/e-mail address | adresa na internetu/E-mail adresa |
| internet connection/wifi | internet prikljucak/WELAN |
| e-mail/file/print | E-mail poštu ispisati |

## LEISURE, SPORTS & BEACH

| | |
|---|---|
| beach/sunshade/lounger | kupalište/suncobran/ležaljka |
| low tide/high tide/current | oseka/plima/struja |
| cable car/chair lift | uspinjaca/lift |
| (rescue) hut/avalanche | (zaštita) sklonište/lavina |

## NUMBERS

| | | | |
|---|---|---|---|
| 0 | nula | 14 | cetrnaest |
| 1 | jedan | 15 | petraest |
| 2 | dva | 16 | šesnaest |
| 3 | tri | 17 | sedamnaest |
| 4 | cetiri | 18 | osamnaes |
| 5 | pet | 19 | devetnaest |
| 6 | šest | 70 | sedamdeset |
| 7 | sedam | 90 | devedeset |
| 8 | osam | 100 | sto |
| 9 | devet | 200 | dvjesto |
| 10 | deset | 1000 | tisucu |
| 11 | jedanaest | 2000 | dvije tisuce |
| 12 | dvanaest | ½ | jedna polovina (pola) |
| 13 | trinaes | ¼ | jedna cetvrtina (cetvrt) |

# ROAD ATLAS

The green line ▬▬▬ indicates the Trips & tours (p. 98–103).
The blue line ▬▬▬ indicates the Perfect route (p. 30–31).

All tours are also marked on the pull-out map

Photo: Krka National Park

# Exploring Dalmatia

**The map on the back cover shows how the area has been sub-divided**

Donji Karin
Corinum
27
Asserin
Benkovac
Benja
Donji
Benkovac
Vrana
Pristeg
13
Banjevci
57
Stankovci
Štane
Vransko
jezero
75
Murter
Tisno
Sovlje
Pirovac
Cista Mala
Prukljansko jezero
Zaton
Skradin
Murter
Murteri
Kaprije
Tijat
Prvić
Žirje
Žirje
Zlarin
Krapanj
Brodarica
Kakan
Zmajan
Žirje
Kakan

Medviđa
Mokro Polje
Padene
Golubić
Radučić
Grad Knin
Kovačić
Topoljskislap
Krčić klanac
Digata
Burnum
509
Macure
Nečman
Manojlovac
Kozjak
1206
Kosovo
Kijevo
Cetina
Kistanje
Sv. Arhanđel
Nacionalni park
Oklaj
Riđane
Vrlika
Ježević
Varvaria
Promona
1148
Rupe
Siritovci
Roški slap
Krka
Visovac
Visovačko jezero
Drniš
Krka
Skradin
Siverić
Otavice
Dom i mauzolej Ivana Meštrovića
61
Maljkovo
Ružić
Umiljanović
Svilaja
1508
Šibenik
Lozovac
Mirlović Zagora
Donje Planjane
Pribude
Gornji Muć
Katedrala sv. Jakova
Rider
542
Vrpolje
Nevest
Gornje Vinovo
Ramljane
55
Perković
Kladnjice
Bršatanovo
Gizdavac
Vrpolje
Primorski Dolac
Brgomet
Boraja
Prapatnica
Kozjak
Vučevica
511
Primošten
Mitlo
738
Kaštel Stari
Kozjak
Salona
Zečevo Rogozničko
Jadranska magistrala
Trogir
Kaštel
Split
Rogoznica
Marina
Vinišće
Sv. Križ
Slatine
Čiovo
Dioklecijanova palača
Solin
Veli Drvenik
Mali Drvenik
Veli Drvenik
Rogač
Splitski kanal
Maslinica
Grohote
Nečujam
Stomorska
Sutivan
Mirca
Mauz. obitelj Petrinović
Šolta
237
Milna
Brač
Ancona
Hvar
Vira
Pescara
Sveti Klement
Vlaka
Hvar
Pakleni otoci
Palmižana
Viški kanal
Oključna
Vis
Vis
Komiža
Podstražje
Biševski
Titova spilja
V. Budikovac
Kamik
346
Svetac
587
117
Zelena spilja
Modra spilja
Polje Biševko
Biševo
kanal

J a d r a n s k o
M o r e

20 km
12.4 mi

Térmoli
Térmoli
Térmoli
Térmoli

239
Sušc

132

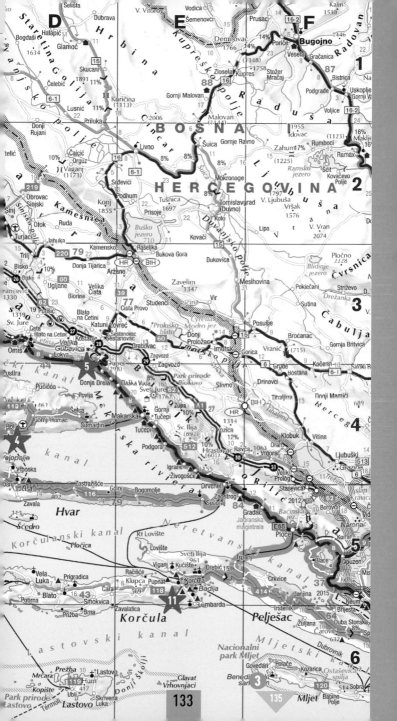

# KEY TO ROAD ATLAS

Autobahn mit Anschlussstellen
Motorway with junctions

Autobahn in Bau
Motorway under construction

Mautstelle
Toll station

Raststätte mit Übernachtung
Roadside restaurant and hotel

Raststätte
Roadside restaurant

Tankstelle
Filling-station

Autobahnähnliche Schnell-
straße mit Anschlussstelle
Dual carriage-way with
motorway characteristics
with junction

Fernverkehrsstraße
Trunk road

Durchgangsstraße
Thoroughfare

Wichtige Hauptstraße
Important main road

Hauptstraße
Main road

Nebenstraße
Secondary road

Eisenbahn
Railway

Autozug-Terminal
Car-loading terminal

Zahnradbahn
Mountain railway

Kabinenschwebebahn
Aerial cableway

Eisenbahnfähre
Railway ferry

Autofähre
Car ferry

Schifffahrtslinie
Shipping route

Landschaftlich besonders
schöne Strecke
Route with
beautiful scenery

Alleenstr. Touristenstraße
Tourist route

XI-V Wintersperre
Closure in winter

Straße für Kfz gesperrt
Road closed to motor traffic

8% Bedeutende Steigungen
Important gradients

Für Wohnwagen nicht
empfehlenswert
Not recommended
for caravans

Für Wohnwagen gesperrt
Closed for caravans

Besonders schöner Ausblick
Important panoramic view

*Wartenstein* Sehenswert: Kultur - Natur
*Umbalfälle* Of interest: culture - nature

Badestrand
Bathing beach

Nationalpark, Naturpark
National park, nature park

Sperrgebiet
Prohibited area

Kirche
Church

Kloster
Monastery

Schloss, Burg
Palace, castle

Moschee
Mosque

Ruinen
Ruins

Leuchtturm
Lighthouse

Turm
Tower

Höhle
Cave

Ausgrabungsstätte
Archaeological excavation

Jugendherberge
Youth hostel

Allein stehendes Hotel
Isolated hotel

Berghütte
Refuge

Campingplatz
Camping site

Flughafen
Airport

Regionalflughafen
Regional airport

Flugplatz
Airfield

Staatsgrenze
National boundary

Verwaltungsgrenze
Administrative boundary

Grenzkontrollstelle
Check-point

Grenzkontrollstelle mit
Beschränkung
Check-point with
restrictions

**ROMA** Hauptstadt
Capital

**VENÉZIA** Verwaltungssitz
Seat of the administration

Ausflüge & Touren
Trips & Tours

Perfekte Route
Perfect route

MARCO POLO Highlight
MARCO POLO Highlight

# INDEX

This index lists all of the places, islands and destinations listed in this guide.
Numbers in bold refer to the main entry.

# WRITE TO US

e-mail: info@marcopologuides.co.uk

Did you have a great holiday?
Is there something on your mind?
Whatever it is, let us know!
Whether you want to praise, alert us
to errors or give us a personal tip –
MARCO POLO would be pleased to
hear from you.
We do everything we can to provide
the very latest information for your trip.

Nevertheless, despite all of our authors'
thorough research, errors can creep
in. MARCO POLO does not accept any
liability for this. Please contact us by
e-mail or post.

MARCO POLO Travel Publishing Ltd
Pinewood, Chineham Business Park
Crockford Lane, Chineham
Basingstoke, Hampshire RG24 8AL
United Kingdom

**PICTURE CREDITS**
Cover photograph: Island Korcul
DuMont Bildarchiv: Kammerhof
65, 70, 74, 75, 77, 83, 85, 86/87
Giovanni Simeone (18/19, 34),
International Centre for Underw
Kora: Ivan Markovic (16 top); K.
Laif: Amme (3 centre bottom, 9
Madej (51, 72), Zahn (2 centre t
bottom); mauritius images: AC
Vujcic (17 top); S. Kuttig (7, 8);
vario images: imagebroker (28

**1st edition 2012**
Worldwide Distribution: Marco
Crockford Lane, Basingstoke, Ha
© MAIRDUMONT GmbH & Co. I
Chief editors: Michaela Lienem
Author: Susanne Sachau; Co-a
Programme supervision: Ann-I
Picture editor: Wieland Hoehn
What's hot: wunder media, Mi
Cartography pull-out map: © I
Design: milchhof : atelier, Berli
Translated from German by Mi
Phrase book in cooperation wi
All rights reserved. No part of t
form or by any means (electro
permission from the publisher
Printed in Germany on non-ch

# DOS & DON'TS

There are a few things you should keep in mind during your visit to Dalmatia

## BATHING WITHOUT SHOES

It is easy to get hurt on the sharp rocks or by treading on a sea urchin on the seabed, so it's better to wear appropriate footwear! If you have been unfortunate enough to tread on a sea urchin, remove the spines immediately with tweezers.

## FIRES

During the hot, dry summer months there is an increased risk of forest fires. From June to October open fires of any kind are not permitted for this reason. Never throw burning objects or glass into the environment. *Report fires immediately (tel. 93)!*

## WHEN THE BORA HITS THE ADRIATIC

A few times during the summer months, but more often during the autumn, the coastline is hit by the bora winds. The sea suddenly changes colour, the offshore wind blows the waves away from the shore, and the temperatures drop rapidly. All boats should immediately seek sheltered bays. Driving a car with a caravan in tow can also be dangerous in this strong wind.

## PARKING ILLEGALLY

Immediately finding a free parking spot on the streets of the towns and holiday resorts during the peak season is akin to winning the lottery. If you do manage to find a place, make sure you're not parking in a no-parking zone. Illegally parked cars are ruthlessly towed away.

## UNDERESTIMATING THE MAIN SEASON

During July and August it is not just the Croats who are on holiday, their neighbours are too. Italians in particular visit Croatia en masse. It is no fun to fight for a spot in overcrowded restaurants and beaches and to pay up to 30 percent more for everything. In addition the clubs and nightclubs also have their peak season at the same time, which means loud music everywhere until the early hours of the morning. If you do not want these things, it is better to avoid the high season.

## SPEEDING IN THE RAIN

When it starts to rain, you should slow down to walking pace: the dust that accumulates during the dry summer weeks turns the roads into slippery surfaces that act like black ice when you try to brake.

## WALKING CROSS-COUNTRY

To this day not all of the areas affected by the Balkan Wars have been cleared of mines. The hinterlands of Zadar and Split are considered dangerous. But you should also avoid leaving the marked trails on the islands, if only because of snakes hiding in the undergrowth.